AN ELUCIDATION OF APPLIED ANATOMY IN *CHARAKA SAMHITA*

Dr. Sakshi

Invincible Publishers

First published in India in 2018 by Invincible Publishers

ISBN: 978-93-87328-38-9

Invincible Publishers

G - 120, Sushant Lok III, Sector 57, Gurgaon-122002

Opposite Kasturba Ashram, Radaur Distt Yamuna Nagar, Haryana- 135133

Printed at Thomson Press India

Dedicated to

My Grandparents

&

My Parents

Dr. S.K.Kaushal & Smt. Sarla Rani

Who stood by me always & guided for my future.

My sister & brothers

For their love & encouragement

My mentors

Late Prof. D.G.Thatee

Dr. Pramod Anand Tiwari

Dr. Rajesh Sharma

PREFACE

This book entitled **"AN ELUCIDATION OF APPLIED ANATOMY IN CHARAKA SAMHITA"** *is a conglomeration of anatomical concepts from Charaka Samhita and its relative comparison with modern applied anatomy. Acharya Charaka was a versatile scholar and knowledgeable human healer.*

The subject Rachna Sharir (Anatomy) is important in studying the morphology but its practical applicability assists the physician to properly diagnose the medical and surgical problem of a patient. The book has been designed with a perspective of providing a basic anatomical concept along with the applied anatomy (including embryological, genetical, topographical, surface, histological and other branches also). Specific signs and symptoms have been mentioned with associated pathology.

Being the Author, this is my first book and I would be grateful to readers to find it useful in academics and clinical review also. I will appreciate and welcome every single and valuable suggestion, improvements from the readers of the book.

Dr . Sakshi

Assistant Professor

Department of Rachna Sharir

ACKNOWLEDGEMENT

On the gracious occasion of the completion of my work I wish to bow my hand and salute with at most reverence to absolute, ultimate and supreme power God.

At this moment I pay my obeisance to my parents ***Dr. S.K.Kaushal & Smt. Sarla Rani*** *whose blessing driven me to achieve the goal of success. Whose pain-taking efforts and never ending love and warmth was the inspiration for me to achieve this task successfully.*

It could be quite impossible for me to complete such a great job without the greatest support and love of my Sister ***Ms. Meenakshi Kaushal*** *and my dear Brothers* ***Mr. Nitin Kaushal & Mr. Naman Kaushal.***

I express profound sense of gratitude with due respect to my teachers ***Dr. P.A.Tiwari, Dr.Jyotsna, Dr.Rajesh Sharma, Dr. Tanvi Mahajan , Dr.Subash Upadhyay*** *and many more to thank for.*

Friends are always supportive at every step of your journey, so I would like to thank my dear friends and colleagues.

INTRODUCTION

Ayurveda is the oldest and immortal system of healing existing since Vedic period. There is no doubt about the treasure of knowledge and principles mentioned in *Ayurveda* about the way of living life. The principles mentioned in contexts of A*yurveda* are mostly philosophical and materialistic and due to this many of the concepts remain unexposed. According to the need of the hour, it is essential to explore the basics of unexposed part of A*yurveda* for the betterment of knowledge.

A traditional view about the origin of *Ayurveda*, elucidates that Lord Brahma imparted this knowledge to *Prajapati Daksha*, who in turn passed it on to the two *Ashwinikumaras*. From *Ashwinikumaras,* this knowledge conceded on to Lord *Indra* and then to Sage *Bhardwaja. Bhardwaja* shared it with other sages; one of them was *Punarvasu Atreya. Atreya* passed it on to his disciples. Based on the knowledge thus imparted, *Agnivesha,* one of *Atreya's* disciples authored a treatise, which came to be known as *Agnivesha-tantra.* This work of *Agnivesha* was revised and enlarged by *Acharya Charaka* around the 5th century A.D. in the form of *Charaka-Samhita.*

Acharya Charaka was one of the principal contributors to the science of medicine and to the art of living. He is known for authoring the medical treatise **"Charaka Samhita".** He is famous as "**The Father of Medicine**". *Acharya Charaka* has mentioned the principle **"prevention is better than cure".**

The word "*Charaka"* states to wandering scholars or physicians. There is some type of controversies related to *Charaka* being a single physician or it refers to a community.

Acharya Charaka describes -

The physician, who is always conversant with the various aspects of the entire body, is very much proficient in the *Ayurveda* that can bring happiness to the universe.

शरीरं सर्वथा सर्व सर्वदा वेद यो भिषक्।
आयुर्वेदं स कात्स्न्येंन वेद लोकसुखप्रदम् ।। (च.शा.6/19)

He contributed to the *Ayurvedic* medicine along with many other fields. He was specialized in fundamental doctrines and unique approach towards the treatment of the diseases. Along with this *Acharya Charaka* stated that a physician who fails to enter the body of a patient with lamp of knowledge and understanding can never treat diseases.

शास्त्रं ज्योतिः प्रकाशार्थं दर्शनं बुद्धिरात्मनः।
ताभ्यां भिषक् सुयुक्ताभ्यां चिकित्सन्नपराध्यति।।(च.सू.9/24)

The physician should be updated with all details of the factors including environment, which influence a patient's disease and then prescription should be done. The concept of *Tridoshas* (*Vata, Pitta,* and *Kapha*) which are responsible for the healthy state in equilibrium and disturbance results in diseased condition of the body. He had a rational approach to causation of disease and its cure. The concept of clinical examination has been mentioned by him.

Charaka Samhita, has been divided into eight *Sthana* (parts) and further sub-divided into 120 chapters. It is an interesting fact that eight parts of A*yurveda* are being touched by *Acharya Charaka* in the *Samhita* in different *Sthana* (parts) and *Adyaya.*

Acharya Charaka discuss about embryology, physiology, pathogenesis and medicine. It was *Acharya Charaka* who put forward for the first time in the medical history, the principles of immunity, metabolism etc. His writings show that he had an insight into genetics also. His knowledge on anatomy and various organs of human body was worth at that period. Specific *Sthana* of the *Samhita* where description of *Sharir,* its parts, sub-parts along with importance, embryology, genetics, is recognized as "*Sharir Sthana*".

Acharya Charaka discussed the fundamental of genetics. For example, he knew about factors determining the sex of *Garbha*. The genetic defects results in physical anomalies. One of the accepted facts in genetics is that the abnormality is present in the gametes and not in the parents. In many of his references, the description about nervous system related diseases like paralysis, facial paralysis, lock-jaw, convulsions etc. are found. He mentioned 360 as total number of bones in human body including teeth also. In relation to division of six major parts, he enumerated fifty-six sub-parts. He counted the number of ligaments, muscles, vital organs, and joints etc which were known by conjecture.

The science of *Ayurveda* is a pool of knowledge which is dynamic and needs to be interpreted by the scholars. The applied anatomy is related to the practical applicability of anatomy. To diagnose or treat a patient, the scholar needs to have knowledge of anatomy and its applied aspects as well as clinical. The mentioned concepts of *Sharir Rachna* in *Charaka Samhita* indicate its applicability in branches like *Kaya Chikitsa, Shalakya, Shalya, Stri- Prasuti Roga* and *Kaumarbhritya.*

With the advancement in the technology and learning aids, the subject "Anatomy" is not only concerned to dissection but its applied aspect is now more appreciated. The entire concept of anatomy in *Ayurveda* is being mentioned in context to *Chikitsa.* To revalidate and explore the anatomical principles we need to study it parallel with the modern anatomy and its applied aspects.

Various branches of anatomy reveal different kind of knowledge like developmental (embryological) anatomy indicates the development of fetus and related congenital defects. The regional (topographic) anatomy is studied in relation to deeper structures. Surface anatomy is an essential branch of regional anatomy that provides information of structures beneath skin and which are perceptible to touch (palpable) in living body at rest and in action. This branch is of paramount importance in physical examination and even for surgery. *Acharya Charaka* has mentioned the surface anatomy & various histological signs at microscopic level without any skilled equipment.

To explore the anatomical aspects mentioned in *Charaka Samhita,* this work has been put forward. *Acharya Charaka* was not only a physician but had knowledge of vital anatomical sites which helped him in proper diagnosis and treatment along with the surgical aspects.

To disperse the misconception that *Acharya Charaka* was merely a good physician and had no proper understanding of anatomy. This fallacy is like a gift of prejudice by a group of good medical fraternity i.e.

" निदाने माधवः श्रेष्ठः सूत्रस्थाने तु वाग्भटः।
शारीरे सुश्रुतःश्रेष्ठश्चरकस्तु चिकित्सिते।।" (वै.सु.)

The subject *Rachna Sharir* is important in studying the morphology but its practical applicability assists the physician to properly diagnose the medical and surgical problem of a patient. *Acharya Charaka* was a versatile scholar and knowledgeable human healer. Through this it will be clearer to apply the concept of applied anatomy in diagnosis and patient care.

CONTENTS

SHARIR SANKHYA SHAARIR

(RELATED TO GENERAL ANATOMICAL FACTS)

Foreword:

In *Ayurvedic* literature, not only *Acharya Sushruta* is considered for his work in area of anatomy or surgery but *Acharya Charaka* is also one of them who also added his work in the pool of knowledge. Being a *Kaya-Chikitsa Pradhna Sampradyic*, he gave much more importance to the *Shaarir* particularly *Rachna Sharir*. In *Shaarir Sthana* of *Charaka Samhita,* he mentioned one separate chapter on *Rachna Sharir*.

In this chapter, he cited the *Shadanga Sharir, Asthi- Santhi, Sira, Dhamani, Snayu, Marma* and *Peshi Sankhya.* There is a combination of many references under this chapter as it comprises the general anatomical structures with their countable numbers. And human gross anatomy is also mentioned for a quick review.

***SHARIR SHADANGATA* :**

तत्रांय शरीरस्याङ्गविभागः; तद्यथा - द्वौ बाहू, द्वे सक्थिनी, शिरोग्रीवम्,

अन्तराधिः, इति षडङ्गमङ्गम्।। (च. शा.7/5)

Acharya Charaka has demonstrated body as 2 बाहू (upper limbs), 2 सक्थिनी (lower limbs), शिरोग्रीवा (head &neck region) and अन्तराधिः (middle body). *Acharya Sushruta* has considered similar body parts with exclusion of (ग्रीवा) neck.

The body is divided into six parts- 2 upper extremities, 2 lower extremities, head, neck and trunk (including chest and abdomen).

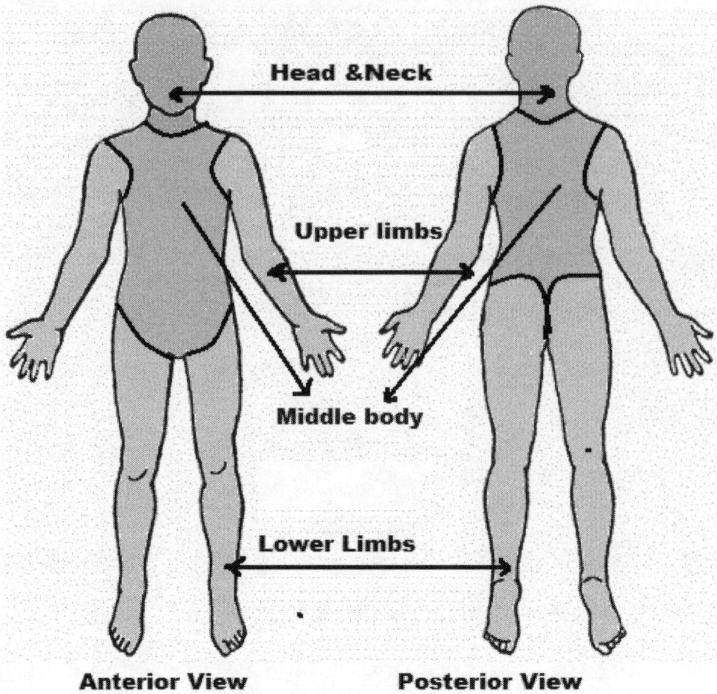

Figure 1.1: Depicting Parts of Body

Acharya Charaka has mentioned types of *Twacha* (skin) with their originating disorders here but for convenience the details are highlighted in separate chapter on *Twacha Sharir*.

There are six layers in the human body as answered by *Lord Atreya* to *Agnivesha* such as- the outermost is the *Udakadhara* (related to water content). The second layer is related to blood, third layer is said to be in relation to origin of *Sidhma* and *Kilasa* diseases, fourth layer has been associated with *Dadru* and *Kustha* . The fifth layer is seat of *Alaji* and *Vidradhi.* The sixth layer when gets injured, causes loss of consciousness and is the seat for origin to boils which are deep rooted on joints and hardly curable. Thus skin covers the entire body along with the six parts.

***ASTHI* (BONES):**

Acharya Charaka has numbered bones as 360 in total. He also included the teeth with their sockets and nails.

त्रीणि सषटीनि शतान्यस्थनां सह दन्तोलूखलनखेन; तद्यथा – द्वात्रिंशद्दन्ताः, द्वात्रिंशद्-दन्तोलूखलानि विंशतिर्नखाः, षष्टिः पाणिपादाङ्गुल्यस्थीनि, विंशतिः पाणिपादशलाकाः, चत्वारि पाणिपाद शलाका धिष्ठानानि, द्वे पाष्ण्र्योरस्थिनी, चत्वारः पादयोर्गुल्फाः, द्वौ मणिकौ हस्तयोःचत्वार्यरत्न्योरस्थनीनिचत्वारि जङ्घयोः, द्वे जानुनी, द्वे जानुकपालिके, द्वावूरुनलकौ, द्वौ बाहुनलकौ, द्वावंसौ, द्वे अंसफलके, द्वावक्षकौ, एकं जत्रु, द्वे तालुके, द्वे श्रोणिफलके, एकं भगास्थि, पञ्चचत्वारिंश-त्पृष्ठगतान्यस्थीनि, पञ्चदश ग्रीवायां, चतुर्दशोरसि, द्वयोः पार्श्वयोश्चतुर्विंशतिः पर्शुकाः तावन्ति स्थालकानि, तावन्ति चैव स्थालकार्बुदानि, एकं हन्वस्थि, द्वे हनुमूलबन्धने, एकास्थि, नासिका-गण्डकूटललाटं, द्वौ शङ्खौ, चत्वारि शिरःकपालानीतिः, एवं त्रीणि सषष्टीनी शतान्यस्थ्नां दन्तोलूखलनखेनेति।। (च. शा.7/6)

They are tabulated as follows:

Sr. No	Name of *Asthi* (bones)	Number of bones	Sr. no	Name of *Asthi* (bones)	Number of bones
1	दन्त (teeth)	32	18	अक्षकास्थि (clavicle)	2
2	दन्तोलूखलनख (teeth sockets)	32	19	जत्रु (sternum)	1
3	नख (nails)	20	20	तालु (palate bone)	2
4	पाणिपादाङ्गुलि- अस्थि (phalangeal bones of hands & feet)	60	21	श्रोणिफलक (hip bones)	2
5	पाणिपादशलाकाएँ (Meta-phalangeal bones of hands & feet)	20	22	भगास्थि (pubis)	1
6	पाणिपादशलाकाधिष्ठान (Meta-phalangeal supports of hands & feet)	4	23	पृष्ठगत अस्थि (vertebrae)	54
7	पार्ष्णि(calcaneum)	2	24	ग्रीवास्थि (cervical bones)	15
8	गुल्फ (ankles)	4	25	उरु- अस्थि (chest)	14
9	मणिबन्ध (wrist)	2	26	पार्श्व की पर्शुकाएं (ribs)	24
10	अरत्नि (fore arms)	4	27	पर्शुकस्थालक (rib- sockets)	24
11	जङ्घास्थि (legs)	2	28	पर्शुकस्थालकार्बुद (tubercl es of ribs)	24
12	जान्वास्थि (knees)	2	29	हन्वस्थि (mandible)	1
13	जानुकपाल (knee-cap)	2	30	हनुमूलबन्धनास्थि (extremeties of mandible)	2
14	उरुनलक (thighs)	2	31	नासिका-गण्डकूटललाट (facial bone)	1
15	बाहुनलक (arms)	2	32	शङ्खास्थि (temporals)	2
16	अंस (shoulders)	2	33	शिर:कपालास्थि (skull bones)	4
17	अंसफलक (shoulder blades)	2		Total number	360

Table: 1.1 Illustrating Number of (*Asthi*) Bones

In modern science (anatomy) the number of bones is around 206. They count it as per the bones in extremities (upper-lower), middle torso, head & neck region.

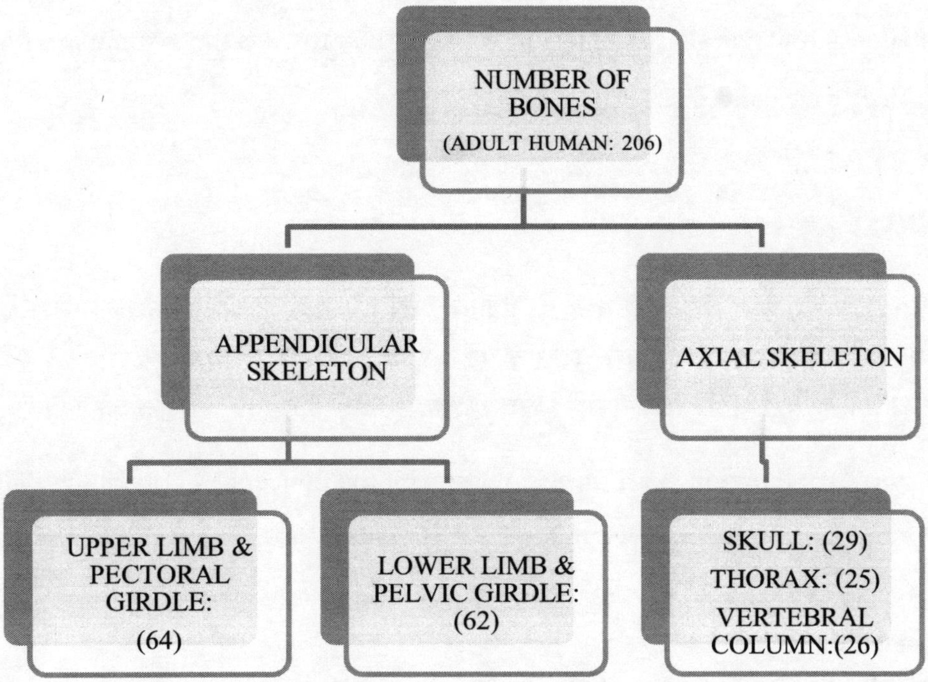

Flowchart1.1: Illustrating Number Of Bones In Modern Anatomy

APPLIED ASPECT OF ASTHI DHATU:

अध्यस्थिदन्तौ दन्तास्थिभेदशूलं विवर्णता।
केशलोमनखश्मश्रुदोषाश्चास्थिप्रदोषजाः।। (च.सू.28/16)

Acharya Charaka has mentioned in the morbidity of *Asthi Dhatu* where he included the disorders like *Adhya Asthi* (extra bone), *Adhi Danta* (teeth over teeth), pain, breaking of *Asthi-Danta*, discolouration, growth of hair, nails is also affected.

According to contemporary science, any extra growth of bony tissue results in discomfort for the patient. It can be related to accessory bones (supernumerary) which develop when additional ossification centers appear and form extra bones. These are most common in foot & should be avoided them as bone fragments in radiographs or medical images.

Similarly there is condition of hyperdontia. These are also known as supernumerary teeth which are present in addition to the normal complement (number) of teeth. They may be single, multiple, erupted-unerupted or arising from both maxilla – mandible bone arches. The commonest are mesiodens(b/w maxillary central incisors). They disturb the normal alignment of dentition and are surgically extracted.

SANKHYA SHARIR:

तद्यथा- नव स्नायुशतानि, सप्त सिराशतानि, द्वे धमनिशते, चत्वारि पेशीशतानि,सप्तोत्तरं मर्मशतं, द्वे सन्धिशते, एकोनत्रिंशत् सहस्त्राणि नव च शतानि षट् पञ्चाशत्कानि सिराधमनीनामणु: प्रविभज्यमानानां मुखागपरिमाणं तावन्ति चैव केशश्मश्रुलोमानीति ।। (च.शा.7/14)

Acharya Charaka has mentioned all these contents by the concept of conjecture. The total number of *Snayu* (ligaments) is 900, *Sira* (veins) is 700, *Dhamani* (arteries) are 200, *Peshi* (muscles) are 400, *Marma* (vital parts) are 107, *Sandhi*(joints) are 200 and further division of blood vessels, hair are about 29956.

Sr. No	Name Of The Part	Total Number
1	***Snayu* (Ligaments)**	**900**
2	***Sira* (Veins)**	**700**
3	***Dhamani* (Arteries)**	**200**
4	***Peshi* (Muscles)**	**400**
5	***Marma* (Vital Parts)**	**107**
6	***Sandhi*(Joints)**	**200**
7	**Division Of Blood Vessels, Hair**	**29956**

Table: 1.3 Showing Total *Sankhya*

The modern anatomy is not dependent upon the classifying the structures on the basis of their number in body. Anatomy is a subject associated to variations at different levels. It may be either linked to number of muscles, veins, nerves etc which may vary due to developmental process. It will be not justified with the two sciences to correlate their concepts at every point. Each science is based on some fundamental aspects which are not subjected to comparison.

***PRATYANGA VIBHAJA NA*:**

षट्पञ्चाशत् पत्यङ्गानि षट्स्वङ्गेषूपनिबद्धानि, यान्यपरिसंख्यातानि पूर्वमङ्गेषु परिसंख्यायमानेषु,
तान्यन्यैः पर्यायैरिह प्रकाशयानि भवन्ति। तद्यथा - द्वे जङ्गापिण्डिके, द्वे ऊरुपिण्डिके, द्वौ स्फिचौ,
द्वौ वृषणौ, एकं शेफः, द्वे उखे, द्वौ वङ्क्षणौ, द्वौ कुकन्दरौ, एकं बस्तिशीर्षम्, एकमुदरं, द्वौ स्तनौ, द्वौ भुजी,
द्वे बाहुपिण्डिकेचिबुकमेंकं, द्वावोष्ठो, द्वे सृक्कण्यौ, द्वौ दन्तवेष्टकौ, एकं तालु, एका गलशुण्डिका, द्वे
उपजिह्विके, एका गोजिह्विका, द्वौ गण्डौ, द्वे कर्णशष्कुलिके, द्वौ कर्णपुत्रकौ, द्वे अक्षिकूटे,चत्वार्यक्षिवर्त्मानि,
द्वे अक्षिकनीतिक, द्वे भ्रवौ, एकाऽवटुः, चत्वारि पाणिपादहृदयानि।।   (च. शा.7/11)

There are fifty –six sub parts of body associated to the six major parts. They have been described as:

Sr. No	Sub parts of body	Number	Sr. No	Sub parts of body	Number
1	जङ्घापिण्डिका (Calves)	2		सृक्कणी (Corners of mouth)	2
2	ऊरुपिण्डिका (Thigh)	2		दन्तवेष्टक (Gums)	2
3	स्फिक (Buttock)	2		तालु (Palate)	1
4	वृषण (Testicles)	2		गलशुण्डिका (Uvula)	1
5	शेफ (Penis)	1		उपजिह्विका (Tonsils)	2
6	उखा (Axilla)	2		गोजिह्विका (Tongue)	1
7	वङ्क्षण(Groin)	2		गण्ड स्थल (Cheeks)	2
8	कुकन्दर (Ischial tuberosities)	2		कर्णशष्कुली (Ear pinnae)	2
9	बस्तिशीर्ष (Pubis)	1		कर्णपुत्रक (Lower ear pinnae)	2
10	उदर (Abdomen)	1		अक्षिकूट (Eye orbit)	2
11	स्तन(Breasts)	2		अक्षिवर्त्म (Eye lids)	2
12	भुजा (Arms)	2		अक्षिकनीनिका (Pupils of eye)	2
13	बाहुपिण्डिका (Fore-arms)	2		अवटु (Thyroid)	1
14	चिबुक (Chin)	1		पाणिपादहृदय (Soles of hands-feet)	4
15	औष्ठ (Lips)	2		Total	56

Table: 1.4 Showing *Pratyanga Vibhajana*

KOSTHANGA:

पञ्चदश कोष्ठाङ्गानि, तद्यथा -नाभिश्च, हृदयं च, क्लोम च, यकृच्च, प्लीहा च, वृक्कौ च, बस्तिश्च, पुरीषाधारश्च, आमाशयश्च, पक्वाशयश्च, उत्तरगुदं च, अधरगुदं च, क्षुद्रान्त्रं च स्थूलान्त्रं च, वपावहनं चेति।। (च. शा.7/10)

The number of visceral organs present in the middle part (*Kostha*) are said to be 15. These are *Nabhi* (navel), *Hridaya* (heart), *Kloma*, *Yakrit* (liver), *Pleeha* (spleen) , *Vrikka* (kidney), *Basti* (urinary bladder), *Purishadara* (caecum), *Aamashya* (stomach), *Pakvashya*(jejunum), Utaraguda (rectum), *Adharaguda* (anus), *Shudrantra* (small intestines), *Sthulaantra* (large intestine) and *Vapavahan* (omentum).

Figure 1.1 below indicates the nine regions of abdomen. Each region comprises of different region along with the organs. This can be related to the *Kosthanga* as mentioned by *Acharya Charaka.* It comprises of basic organs associated with digestion process. Here comes the difference in opinion of the concepts of two sciences.

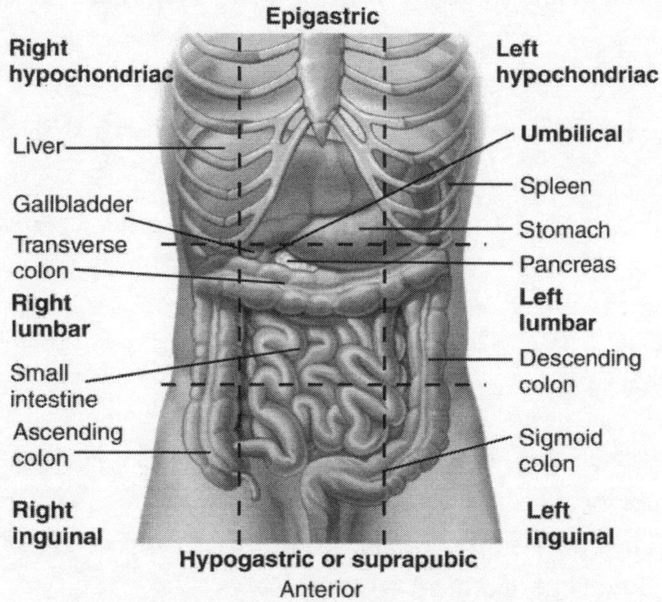

Figure 1.1 Showing Nine Regions Of Abdomen

PRAMANA SHARIR:

Acharya Charaka while describing the tenfold examination of patient (*Dasavidha Atura Pariksha*) told *Pramana Sharir* which is unique way which has definite measurements in the form of *Anguli Pramana.*

प्रमाणतश्चेति, शरीरप्रमाणं पुनर्यथास्वेनाङ्गुलिप्रमाणेनोपदेक्ष्यते उत्सेधविस्तारायामैर्यथा- क्रमम्। तत्र पादौ चत्वारि षट् चतुर्दशाङ्गुलानि, जङ्घे त्वष्टादशाङ्गुले षोडशाङ्गुल परिक्षेपे च, जानुनी .... षडङ्गुलदीर्घौ वृषणावष्टाङ्गुलपरिणाहौ, शेफः षडङ्गुलदीर्घं ....केवलं पुनः शरीरमङ्गुलिपर्वाणि चतुरशोतिः। तदायामविस्तारसमं सममुच्यते। तत्रायुर्बलमोजः सुखमैश्वर्यं वित्तमिष्टाश्चापरे भावा भवन्त्यायत्ताः प्रमाणवति शरीरे। विपर्ययस्त्वतो हीनेऽधिक वा।। (च. वि.8/117)

The measurement of the body (anthropometry) will be described by the measure of individual fingers in terms of height, breadth and length respectively. Measurements for different body parts are mentioned by *Acharya Charaka*. The entire body measures eighty four fingers in height and also in breadth (extended arms). The persons having normal measurement of the body are endowed with longevity, strength, immunity, happiness, supremacy, wealth and other desired qualities. Those having body with less or more measurement have qualities contrary to those. [9]

Understanding of *Pramana Sharir* in the present era can help in the making of artificial limbs, so that the measurement of artificial limbs can be estimated from the stature of the person.

In modern science *Pramana Sharir* is correlated with anthropometry which is useful for physical measurements in order to assess height, age, sex etc. It is an integral part of forensic science as it helps in identifying the individuals.

KEYS POINTS:

- It deals with the basic concepts of General Anatomy as per mentioned in the classical text of *Charaka Samhita*.
- The body is divisible into four limbs (upper- lower), middle body (chest & abdomen) and head –neck region.
- *Acharya Charaka* has mentioned the different types of *Twacha* which more or less can be related to the modern skin types. In addition to this, there is reference of *Kosthanga* (organs in abdomino- pelvic region).
- There are facts related to the number of bones with the applied aspect also. Along with this he has mentioned the countable number of *Snayu, Dhamani, Sira, Peshi* and *Pratyanga* many more.
- *Pramana Sharir* has clinical relation in case of forensic sciences, artificial limbs fixation etc.

<u>GARBHA SHARIR AND ANUVANSHIKI</u> (EMBRYOLOGY & GENETICS)

Introduction:

The knowledge of *Sharir* begins with the knowledge of *Garbha*. The importance of *Garbha Sharir* lies in understanding the concept of conception from beginning till birth. It helps in better attainment of a healthy child which further helps in development of healthy society. The subject is concerned with the normal development and knowing the factors related to the abnormality of the developing foetus. This chapter deals with the essential factors for development of *Garbha* (fetus), genetically review along with the malformations involved at different levels.

The concept of **genetics** told by *Acharya Charaka* is as follows.

शरीरावयवास्तु परमाणुभेदेनापरिसंख्येया भवन्ति, अतिबहुत्वादतिसौक्ष्म्यादतीन्द्रियत्वाच्च।

तेषां संयोग विभागे परमाणूनां कारणं वायुः कर्मस्वभावष्च।। (च.शा.7/17)

According to *Acharya Charaka*, human body is a congregation of *Aparisankhya* (millions & billions) of *Deha Pramanu* which means they are innumerable and uncountable. The concept of " सृष्टि उत्पत्ति क्रम " (evolution) is being stated by *Acharya Charaka* and *Acharya Sushruta*. It is also a known fact that " यत् पिण्डे तत् ब्रह्माण्डे" which states that whatever body comprises of, is also present in the universe. *Acharya Charaka* has mentioned many useful couplets concerning role of paternal and environmental imprinting in *Ayurveda*. These appear more towards theoretical side but they are clinically much important. In the history of *Ayurveda* the concept of *Beeja*, *Beeja Bhaga*, *Beeja Bhagavayava* and *Beeja Bhagavayava Dosha* postulated by *Acharya Charaka* was a great breakthrough in the history of medical world.

The transmission of characters /traits from parents to child and along with generations is called as *Anuvanshiki* (inheritance). These are being transferred by the *Beeja* (ovum-sperm) *Beeja Bhaga* (chromosomes) and *Beejabhagavayaya* (genes). Gene is the principal unit of inheritance. *Matraj* and *Pitraj bhava* can be related with the parental imprints. The mutations which occur in genes (known as genetic mutation) lead to different types of congenital anomalies. The *Beejabhaga* and *Beejbhagavayava* described are similar to chromosome &genes concept of modern science. Various genetic diseases are developed due to any deformity in the *Beejabhaga*, *Beejbhagavayava*. These factors also carry same type of deformity in next generation. The study of *Beeja* and *Beejbhaga*, *Beejdosha* is useful for *Supraja* (healthy offspring) and to cure various congenital diseases.

The term **genetics** is defined as the study of genes and their hereditary value. In view of clinical aspect it is the application of genetics to diagnose genetic disorders and patient care. The developmental genetics is the branch of genetics concerned with how development is controlled by specific genes.

The term **embryology** is the science of origin and development of the individual from fertilization of an oocyte to the end of the embryonic and fetal period. In textbook of human embryology, it is the study of the formation and development of the embryo (or fetus) from the moment of its inception up to the time when it is born as an infant.

CONCEPT OF BEEJA:

बीज के पर्याय: **जीवाणु, तत्त्व, मूल, स्त्रोत, कारण**

The word „*Beeja*" refers to *Jeevanu, Tatva, Moola* (root), *Karna* (cause). It is the basic necessity of a new beginning (here in reference to an individual). *Beeja* (ovum-sperm) are the factors responsible for the development of a fetus. All healthy features of *Beeja* will produce a healthy offspring.

बीजं हि स्वसदृश्यमड्कुरं करोति.... (च.शा.2/35)चक्रपाणि टीका

According to *Chakrapani*, *Beeja* is the main cause of *Utpatti Beejam* (seed), which has the capacity to induce new growth / generation.

SHUKRA (SEMEN):

The *Purush Beeja* (male gamete cell) in *Ayurveda* is identified with eligibility to cause *Garbha* is known as *Shukra* (semen).

Etymology:

In *Manu Smiriti,* with reference *to Virya,* the word *Shukra* is used.

वीर्य-पुमान् पुंसोऽधिके शुक्रे स्त्री भवत्यधिके स्त्रिया: (मनु0 3/69,5/63)

शुक्र के पयाय (Synonyms): वीर्य, रेतस, पुंबीज

In *Ayurveda,* the *Purush Beeja* (sperm/semen) represents with the following features that are similar to the male gamete cell that is capable of producing offspring.

शुक्रं तदस्य प्रवदन्ति धीरा यद्धीयते गर्भसमुद्भवाय।

वाय्वग्निभूम्यब्गुणपादवत्तत् षड्भ्यो रसेभ्यः प्रभवश्य तस्य।। **(च. शा.2/4)**

The wise call it as "*Shukra"(*Semen/Sperm*)* which is implanted for the origin of *Garbha* .It is constituted of four quarters of *Vayu, Agni, Prithvi* and *Aapa* (Four *Mahabhutas*) and is originated from six *Rasas.*

बहलं मधुरं स्निग्धमविस्रं गुरू पिच्छिलम्।

शुक्लं बहु च यच्छुक्रं फलवत्तदसंशयम्।। (च.चि.2.4.50)

The normal and healthy *Purush Beeja* (sperm) is attributed with viscous, sweet, unctuous quality, devoid of unpleasant smell, heavy, slimy and abundant.

स्निग्धं घनं पिच्छिलं च मधुरं चाविदाहि च।

रेतः शुद्धं विजानियाच्छ्वेतं स्फटिकसन्निभम्।। (च.चि.30.145)

It also has non- burning and white like rock crystal properties & should be taken as pure (normal).

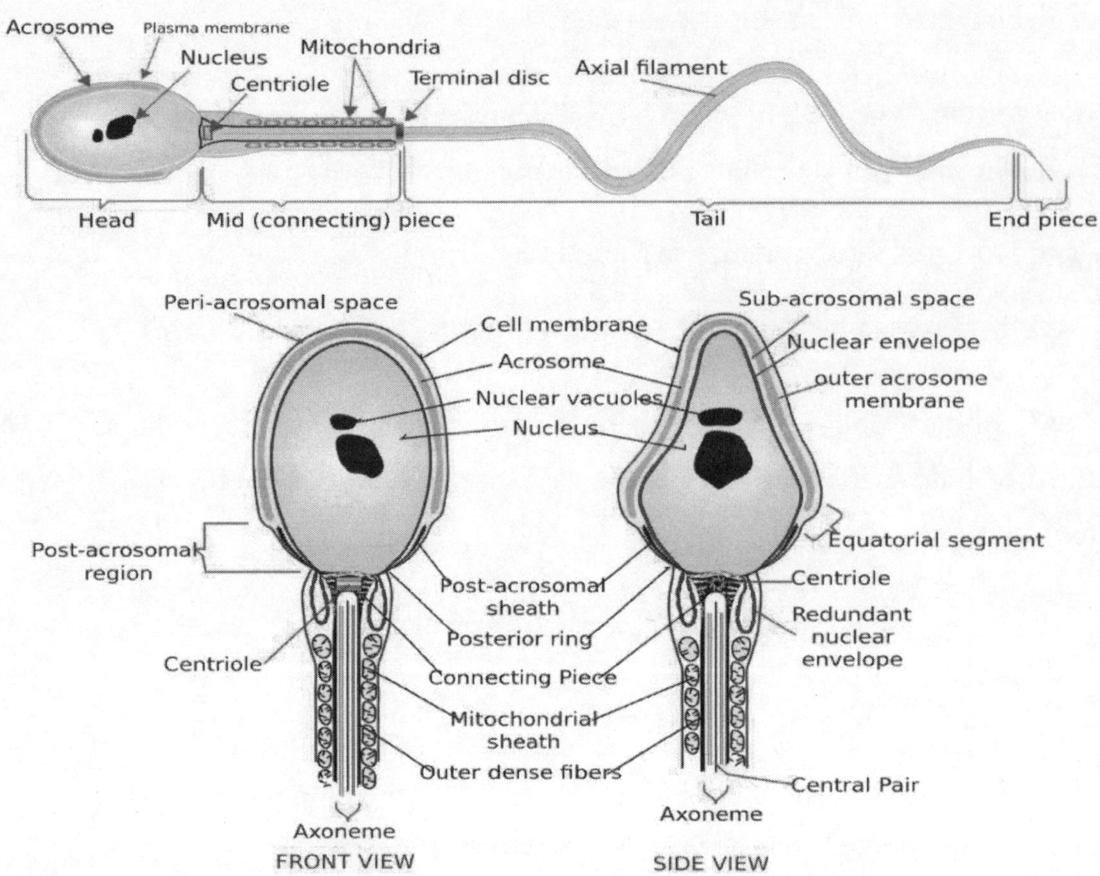

Fig: 2.1 Normal Structure of Sperm Cell

Normal Structure of Sperm:

A normal spermatozoon is highly specialized, free swimming actively motile cell. It has a head, neck, middle piece and principal piece or tail.

- ***Head***: it is piriform shape, 4µm in length. It is derived from nucleus which consists of 23 highly condensed chromosomes. An important structure here is acrosomic cap. *Function:* Nucleus contain genetic information and half number of chromosomes. The acrosome releases a hyaluronidase enzyme which destroys the hyaluronic acid of the ovum and enters into the ovum.
- ***Neck:*** funnel-shaped basal body, a spherical centriole. It is known as connecting piece as it connects head and remainder of spermatozoa. *Function:* Distal centriole gives rise to axial filament of the sperm which runs up to the end of the tail.
- ***Axial filament:*** the point where the middle piece joins the tail, axial filament passes through a ring like structure called annulus. *Function:* Middle piece is called power house of sperm

because it gives energy to the sperm to swim in the female genital tract. Tail helps the sperm to swim in the female genital tract. It is the main part of sperm to move.

Spermatozoa acquire the ability to fertilize an ovum only after they have been in the female genital tract for some time. This final step in their maturation is called as "Capacitation". Semen quality is a means of ability of semen to accomplish fertilization.

Properties of Semen:

The good quality semen comprises of following features:

S. No	Characteristics	Normal range
1.	Specific gravity	1.028
2.	Volume	2-6ml/ejaculation
3.	Reaction	pH of 7.5 (alkaline). The alkalinity due to prostatic secretions.
4.	Sperm count	Must be at least 20 millions/ ml & sperms should be 40 millions.

Table: 2.1 Illustrating Properties of Semen

Abnormalities of *Shukra*:

The normal *Shukra* (sperm) causes a variety of deformities when vitiated by *Tri Doshas*.

फेनिलं तनु रूक्षं च विवर्णं पूति पिच्छिलम्।अन्यधातूपसंसृष्टमवसादि तथाऽष्टमम्।। फेनिलं तनु रूक्षं च कच्छेणाल्पं च मारूतात्। भवत्युपहतं शुक्रं न तद्गर्भाय कल्पते। सनीलमथवा पीतमत्युष्णं पूतिगन्धि च। दहल्लिङ्गं विनिर्याति शुक्रं पित्तेन दूषितम्। श्लेष्मणा बद्धमार्गं तु भवत्यत्यर्थपिच्छिल्लम्।। स्त्रीणामत्यर्थगमना दभिघातात् क्षतादपि। शुक्रं प्रवर्तते जन्तोःप्रायेण रूधिरान्वयम्।। वेगसन्धारणाच्छुक्रं वायुना विहतं पथि। कृच्छ्रण याति ग्रथितमवसादि तथाऽष्टमम्।। इति दोषाः समाख्याताः शुक्रस्याष्टौ सलक्षणाः।।

(च. चि.30.139-144)

When vitiated due to *Vata* the *Shukra* (semen) becomes frothy, thin and loses its stickiness. The volume of *Shukra* decreases and semen becomes thin. Here the sperm count gets affected. In case of *Pittaj Shukra (*semen) it looks yellow in color and has offensive odour. The ejaculation is accompanied by the burning sensation in penis. The vitiated *Kapha*, results in increased stickiness of semen and takes time to liquefy. The motility rate is reduced . Sometimes due to injury in genital tract and increased sexual activity the semen is afflicted with the blood stain. When *Vata* aggravates due to suppression of sexual urge it causes clumping of semen and is known as "*Avasadi*".

शुक्रस्य दोषात् क्लैब्यमहर्षणम्। रोगो वा क्लीबमल्पायुर्विरूपं वा प्रजायते।।
न चास्य जायते गर्भः पतति प्रस्रवत्यपि। शुक्रं हि दुष्टं सापत्यं सदारं बाधते नरम्।।
(च . सू. 28/18-19)

In concept of disorders caused due to morbidity of *Shukra Dhatu* (semen) there is presence of impotency and non-erection of penis. His progeny will be short lived or deformed. There are little chances of conception and if conceived, it may be miscarried or aborted.

The commentary by *Acharya Chakrapani* interprets „*Kailabya*" as non-erection of penis and „*Aharsana*" as incapability in sexual act but the variant looks appropriate when the position is quite reverse. The absence of *Shishno-Uthana,* in ability in coitus, here is the reference to *Kailabya, Alpaayu, Viroopa Santana* & even condition of abortion may occur. *Acharya Gangadhara* perhaps takes both as one condition.

Abnormalities of Sperm:

The structure of a sperm can be different from the normal one due to many reasons. Sperm sometimes due to various defects shows morphological changes. The abnormal represents with double head, large or small deformed head. The tail part also shows double flagellum which affects it motility.

The sperm cell sometimes represents double head or tail, size of the cell may vary. Spermatozoa may be too large (giant) or too small (dwarf). The head, body, or tail may be duplicated.

The defects in sperm cell relating to head must be less than 35%, middle piece defect must be less than 20% and tail defects less than 20%.

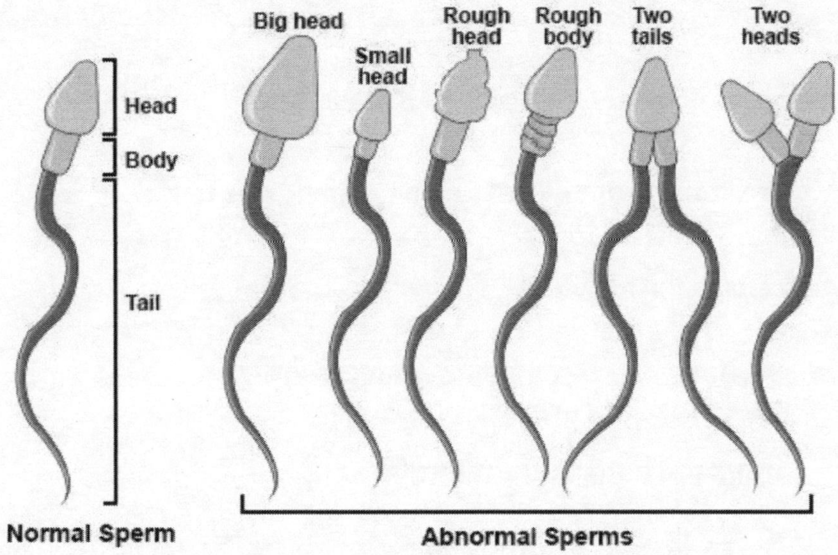

Fig: 2.2 Showing Structural Abnormalities of Sperm Cell

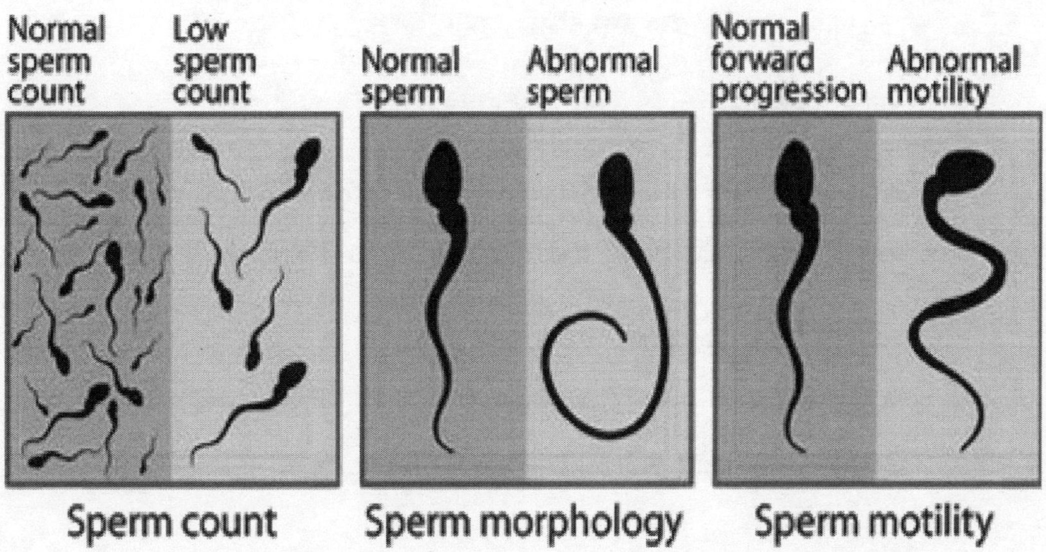

Fig: 2.3 Showing Morphological Abnormalities of Sperm

SHONITA/ ARTAVA (OVUM):

The *Stri Beeja* (female gamete cell) in *Ayurveda* that is responsible for fertilization is known as *Aartava* or *Shonita.* There are references from text which relate to the *Stri beeja.*

Etymology:

The word *Shonita* is derived from (शोण) prefix and (इतच्) *Prtaya*

शोणित - (शोण + इतच्) लाल, लोहित, रक्त वर्ण

The *"Shonita"* word refers to the red color.

आर्तव के पयाय (Synonyms): रज, आर्तव, शोणित,स्त्रीबीज

मासान्निष्पिच्छदाहार्ति पञ्चरात्रानुबन्धि च।

नैवातिबहु नात्यल्पमार्त्तवं शुद्धमादिशेत्। (च. चि.30.225)

The normal and healthy *Stri Beeja* (ovum or menstrual discharge) should be taken as normal menstrual discharge which comes forth monthly without sliminess, burning sensation, pain, stays for five days and in quantity is neither too much nor to little.

गुञ्जाफलसवर्णं च पद्मालक्तकसन्निभम्।

इन्द्रगोपकसङ्काशमार्तवं शुद्धमादिशेत्।। (च. चि.30.226)

When the ovum is not fertilized only then it is shed off from body as menstrual discharge . In color, normal menstrual blood should be similar to *Gunja* fruit, red lotus flower, *Indragopaka* (red insect).

According to *Acharya Chakrapani Shonita* term is similar to *Artava.* And he also stated that *Artava* is also affected by the same factors as that of semen.

Normal Structure of Ovum:

Ova develop from the oogonia present in the cortex of ovary. The oogonia are surrounded by other cells that form the stroma. These stromal cells form ovarian or graffian follicles that surround ova and protect them.

Following are the stages:

- Some cells of stroma become flattened and surround an oocyte. These cell forms the follicular cells.

- These flattened cells later become columnar. Follicles up to this stage develop into primordial follicle. A homogeneous membrane, the zona pellucida appears between follicle cells and oocyte.
- The follicular cells proliferate to form several layers. They are known as membrane granulose or granulosa cells.
- An antrum appears within membrana granulosa and a follicle appears with its appearance. This cavity increases in size and walls of follicle become thin. The oocyte eccentrically surrounded by the granulose cells (cumulus oophoricus or cumulus ovaricus). The cells that attach to the wall are called as discus proligerus.
- As the follicle expands, the stromal cells become condensed and form a thick coverig theca interna. They secrete the oestrogen hormone.
- Outside the theca interna some fibrous tissue condensed to form another covering for the follicle called theca interna.

Ovum is surrounded by zona pellucida. Some cells of corona radiate can be seen sticking outside of zona pellucida. The nuclear membrane has dissolved for second meiotic division. The first polar body lies in pre vettiline space. Ovum is a very large cell and measures more than 100 μm in diameter.

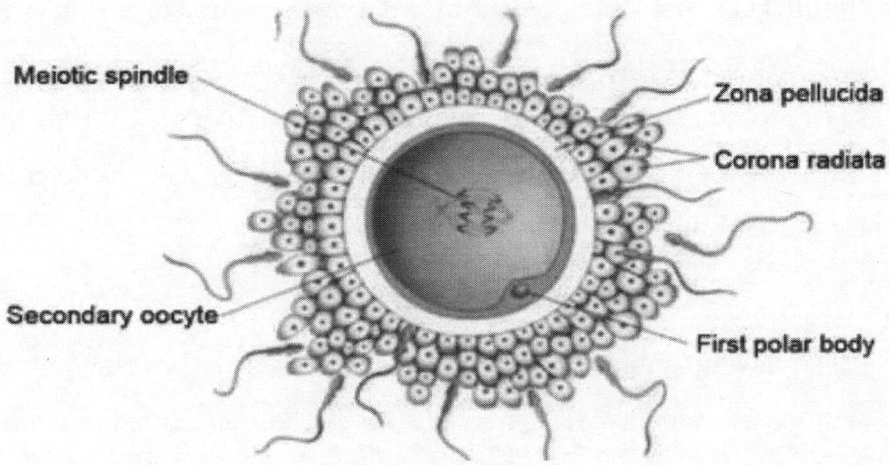

Fig: 2.4 Showing Normal Structure of Ovum

The **abnormal form** of ovum represent with the unusual large nucleus or two nuclei. Two oocytes may be seen in one follicle.

BEEJA BHAGA (CHROMOSOMES):

The chromosome is a structure in the nucleus consisting of chromatin and carrying genetic information for the cell. The number of chromosome for each cell is fixed for every species and in human it is forty-six. Chromosomes in humans can be divided into two types: autosomes (body chromosome(s) and allosome (sex chromosome (s).

Certain genetic traits are linked to a person's sex and are passed on through the sex chromosomes. The autosomes contain the rest of the genetic hereditary information. All act in the same way during cell division. Human cells have 23 pairs of chromosomes (22 pairs of autosomes and one pair of sex chromosomes), giving a total of 46 per cell. In addition to these, human cells have many hundreds of copies of the mitochondrial genome. Sequencing of the human genome has provided a great deal of information about each of the chromosomes.

Factors for Hereditary Defects:

यच्चोक्तं - यदि च म्नष्यो मनुष्यप्रभवः, कस्मान्न जडादिभ्यो जाताः पितृसदृशरूपा भवन्तीति; तत्रोच्यते -यस्य यस्य ह्यङ्गवायवस्य बीजे बीजभाग उपतप्तो भवति तस्य तस्याङ्गावयवस्य विकृतिरुपजायते, उपजायते चानुपतापातु; तस्मादुभयोपपत्तिरप्यत्र। सर्वस्य चात्मजानीन्द्रियाणि, तेषा भावाभावहेतुर्दैवं तस्मान्नैकान्ततो जडादिभ्यो जाताः पितृसदृशरूपा भवन्ति।। (च.शा.3/17)

The concept of fertilization and development of embryo is discussed, it is also included that a man is born from man but the offspring is not similar. If the abnormality results, it is due to the damaged genetic source of that part. And if nothing happens like this no such case is observed. He said that sense organs are self derived and their presence/absence is determined by fate. So offspring are not invariably similar to parents.

As per *Acharya Chakrapani"s* view the genes carry the genetic basis of all the body parts and thus produce the person having similar body parts but the senses are governed by the deed enshrined in the soul. Thus even in patients of leprosy, the disease is transmitted to the offspring only if the genes are affected otherwise not. On the other hand, in case of senses, it is only by chance that the offspring of a blind man comes as blind.

Here the term "*Beeja*" refers to both male & female gamete cell. The similarity or dissimilarity to father is determined by the *Aatmaja Bhava* .

The above mentioned view of *Acharya Charaka* can be correlated with the modern embryological view point on the same. The chromosome factor plays important role in explaining the fact for similarity and dissimilarity among two individuals.

No Two Persons Are Alike:

This fact can be better explained under concept of second meiotic division. Here the diploid number of chromosomes is restored (46). So it provides consistency of chromosome number from generation to generation.

During the first meiotic division, chromosomes derived from the parents are distributed between daughter cells entirely at random. Along with phenomenon of crossing over results in thorough shuffling of genetic material, so they have a distinct genetic content. A third step in process of genetic material shuffling takes place at fertilization when there is combination of randomly selected spermatozoa and ova. It is, therefore, not two persons are alike (except identical twins).

Causes of Deformity in a Female Child:

यतस्तु कात्स्न्र्येनाविनश्न् विकृतिमापद्यते, तदनुव्याख्यास्यामः ,यदा स्त्रिया दोषप्रकोपणा- न्यासेवमानाया दोषाः प्रकुपिताः शरीरमुपसर्पन्तः शोणितगर्भाशयावुपद्यन्ते, न च कात्स्न्र्येन शोणित- गर्भाशयौ दूषयन्ति, तदेयं गर्भं लभते स्त्री; ....यस्य यस्य ह्यवयवस्य बीजे बीजभागे वा दोषाः प्रकोपमापद्यन्ते, तं तमवयमं विकृतिराविशति। यदा ह्यस्याः शोणिते गर्भाशयबीजभागः प्रदोषमापद्यते तदा वन्ध्यांजनयति; यदा पुनरस्याः शोणिते गर्भाशयबीजभागावयवः प्रदोषमाद्यते, तदा पूतिप्रजां जनयति; .... स्त्र्याकृतिभूयिष्ठामस्त्रियं वार्तां नाम जनयति, तां स्त्रीव्यापदमाचक्षते।। (च.शा.4.30)

The hereditary defect that occurs in fetus is due to the imperfection of *Beeja*, *Beeja Bhaga* and *Beejabhagavayava.*

If the woman conceived when her ovum and uterus were not completely vitiated but simply afflicted by the circulating *Doshas.* The organs, derived from the maternal source (ovum) like; skin, blood etc. gets deformed. These vitiated *Doshas* may afflict the *Beeja* (chromosomes) or *Beeja Bhaga* (genes) from where the organs derived gets deformed. When the *Beejabhaga* in the ovum of mother which is responsible for the production of uterus is

excessively vitiated, then she gives birth to a sterile child. When the *Beejabhagavayava* is vitiated due to *Doshas* then she gives birth to *Putipraja.*

When *Beejabhagavayava* which is responsible for the production of the uterus and also portion of *Beejabhaga* which are responsible for the organs that characterize a female like breasts, genital organs, hair etc; in the ovum of the mother gets excessively vitiated then she gives birth to a child who is not a complete female but only with characteristics- such type of child is known as *Varta. Acharya Chakrapani* states that " गर्भाशयबीजभागावयव

means, a portion of the genes producing uterus or both uterus and ovum.

Similarly, in the reference to the *Yonivyapada* 30th chapter (Chikitsa Sthana) among 20 disorders the case of *Suchimukhi* and *Sandhya yoni* fall under the category of genetical defects.

गर्भस्थायाः स्त्रिया रौक्ष्याद् वायुर्योनिं प्रदूषयन्।

मातृदोषादणुद्वारां कुर्यात् सूचीमुखी तु सा।। (च. चि.30.31)

In female fetus, *Vata* due to roughness affects the genital tract and produce minute opening caused by maternal (genetic) defect and this condition is called as *Suchimikhi.*

बीजदोषात्तु गर्भस्थमारूतोपहताशया।

नृद्वेषिण्यस्तनी चैव षण्ढी स्यादनुपक्रमा।। (च. चि.30.34)

And in condition of *Sandhya yoni*, if genetic defect persists, in female fetus the *Vata* destructs the ovary; the woman has aversion to males and devoid of breasts. The secondary development is affected.

Causes of Deformity in Male Child:

एवमेव पुरूषस्य यदा बीजे बीजभागः प्रदोषमापद्यते, तदा वन्ध्यं जनयति; यदा पुनरस्य बीजे बीजभागावयवः प्रदोषमाद्यते, तदा पूतिप्रजं जनयति; यदा त्वस्य बीजे बीजभागावयवः पुरूषकाराणां च शरीरबीजभागानामे कदेशः प्रदोषमापद्यते, तदा पुरूषाकृतिभूयिष्ठामपुरूषं तृणपुत्रिकं नाम जनयति, तां पुरूषव्यापदमाचक्षते। (च.शा.4.31)

As similar to the female child deformity, when the part of the *Beeja* which is responsible for the production of the sperm in the fetus is excessively vitiated, then this gives birth to a sterile child. When the *Beejabhagavayava* which is responsible for the production of the sperm is excessively vitiated, then it results in birth to a *Putipraja*. When *beejabhagavayava* which is responsible for the production of sperm and also portions of the *Beejabhaga* which are responsible for the production of organs that characterize a male, are excessively vitiated, then this gives birth to a child who is not a complete male but only having masculine characteristics and is known as *Tranaputrika*.

यथा बीजमकालाम्बुकृमिकीटाग्नि दूषितम्।

न विरोहति संदुष्टं तथा शुक्रं शरीरिणाम्।। (च.चि.30.134)

Acharya Charaka quoted an example that a seed (of a plant) does not sprout if affected by water, worm , insects, improper time and fire so is the defective semen of man and this explains the deformity in a male

Chromosomal Deformity (Modern Correlation):

The chromosomal abnormalities may be in number or it can be structural.

Numerical abnormality:

It is due to an abnormal number of chromosomes. It consists of aneuploidy and polyploidy types. These can be further sub divided into monosomy, triosomy, tetrasomy or pentasomy etc. like as an individual is missing either a chromosome from a pair (monosomy) or has more than 2 chromosomes of a pair (triosomy).

Structural abnormality:

When the structure of chromosome gets modified due to many factor. It can be of following types:

- Deletion: part of a chromosome may be lost for example in case of Wolf Hirschhorn syndrome (arm of chromosome 4 is deleted).
- Translocation: part of a chromosome may get attached to a chromosome of a different pair. Here chromosome number 13, 14,15,21,22 are affected.
- Duplication: the two chromosomes of a pair may break at unequal distances. When each piece joins the opposite chromosome, one chromosome is longer than the normal and some of the genes get duplicated. The chromosome will be shorter than normal, some genes being missing. For example: Charcot Marie tooth disease type 1A (chromosome 17 affected).
- Inversion: a piece separating from a chromosome may get inverted before joining the opposite chromosome.

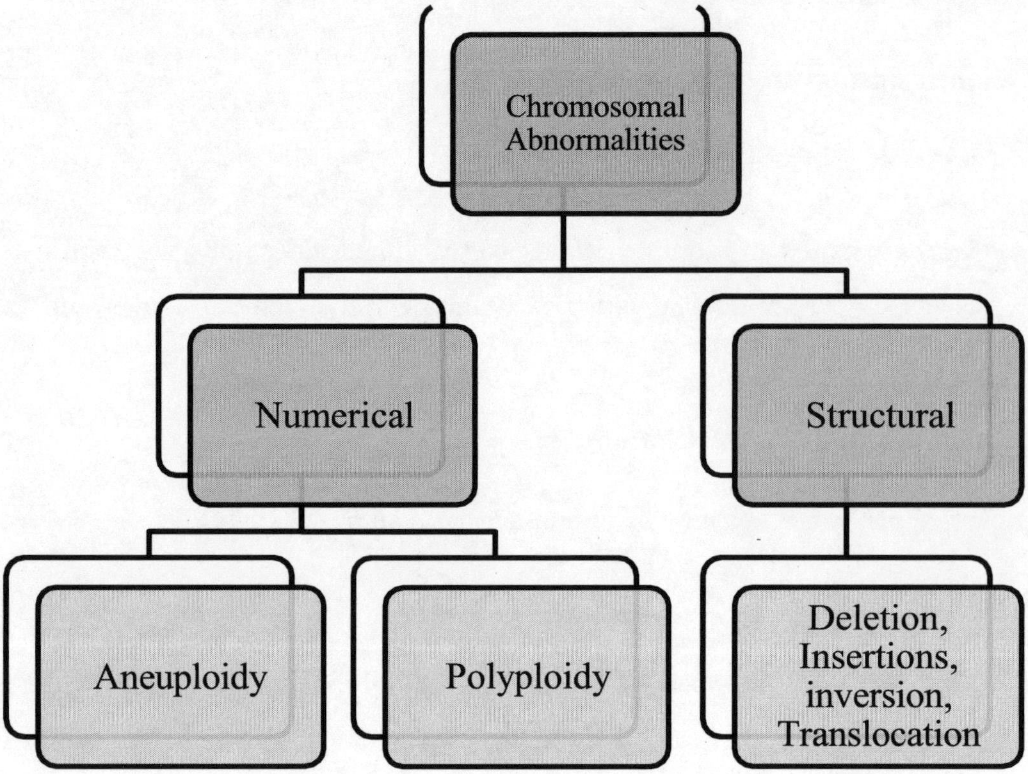

Flowchart: 2.1 Classifications of Chromosomal Deformity

Concept of Triosomy:

At time of fertilization by this gamete, the zygote will, therefore, have 47 chromosomes; there being three identical chromosomes instead of one of the normal pairs and called as Trisomy. Below is given an example of triosomy.

Mongolism or Down's syndrome: Trisomy of chromosome 21 results in a condition called Mongolism or Down"s syndrome.

The syndrome has following clinical features:

Child has a broad face, oblique palperable fissures, epicanthus, a furrowed lower lip and broad hands with a single transverse crease. The patients are mentally retarded and mostly have heart anomalies.

Presence of Extra Chromosome:

The presence of an extra X or Y chromosome can result in different syndromes with mental retardation and abnormal growth. Following are included:

- XXX (Abnormal Female)

They are sometimes referred as Super females. There body development is poor (sexual development i.e. infantile) and menstruation is scanty.

- XXY (Abnormal Male/ Klinefelter‟s Syndrome)

The subject is a male because of presence of Y chromosome. The testes are poorly developed leading to the sterility and gynecomastia.

- XYY(Abnormal Male)

When both chromosomes of a pair go to one gamete, the other gamete resulting from the division has only 22 chromosomes (instead of 23); and at fertilization the zygote has 45 chromosomes. So it is called as Monosomy where one pair is represented by single chromosome.

Turner's syndrome:

Turner‟s syndrome is an example of this female with only one X chromosome. Here subject is always a female. There is agenesis of ovaries and associated deformities include mental retardation, skeletal abnormalities and folds of skin on side of neck (webbed neck).

All these modern correlation with following syndromes (related to chromosomes) have been observed under the perception of *Beeja, Beejabhaga* and *Beejabhagavayava.*

<table>
<tr><th colspan="3">Table 1. Chromosome Abnormalities and Disease</th></tr>
<tr><th colspan="2">Chromosome Abnormality</th><th>Disease Association</th></tr>
<tr><td rowspan="8">X, Y</td><td>XO</td><td>Turner's Syndrome</td></tr>
<tr><td>XXY</td><td>Klinefelter syndrome</td></tr>
<tr><td>XYY</td><td>Double Y syndrome</td></tr>
<tr><td>XXX</td><td>Trisomy X syndrome</td></tr>
<tr><td>XXXX</td><td>Four X syndrome</td></tr>
<tr><td>Xp21 deletion</td><td>Duchenne's /Becker syndrome, congenital adrenal hypoplasia, chronic granulomatus disease</td></tr>
<tr><td>Xp22 deletion</td><td>steroid sulfatase deficiency</td></tr>
<tr><td>Xq26 deletion</td><td>X-linked lymphproliferative disease</td></tr>
</table>

Table: 2.2 Different Chromosomal DeformitiesTable:

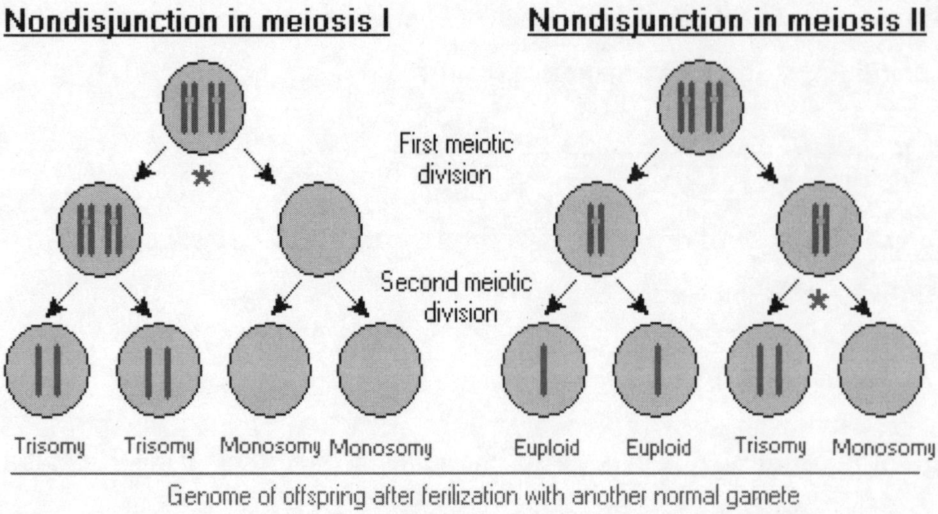

Fig: 2.5 Showing Non- Disjunctions In Meiosis I-II

GARBHA (EMBRYO FORMATION):

Etymology:

In *Vachispatyama,* the word *"Garbha"* is described as

गृ- भनृ वा द्वित्वे भस्य बः। (वा.)

In *Shabada Kalpa Druma*, the reference in context to *Garbha* is mentioned.

- गीर्य्यते जीवसचित कर्मफलदात्रा ईश्वरेण प्रकृति बलात् जठर गड्करे स्थाप्यते
  पुरूष शुक्रयोगेनासौ (श.क.द्रु.भाग2)

***Atulya Gotra* (Marriage in the different Clan):**

The concept of marriage in different clan has been mentioned centuries ago by the *Ayurvedic* scholars. They knew this fact that the diseases which are carried by the genes from one generation to the other result in occurrence of disease.

अतुल्यगोत्रस्य रजःक्षयान्ते रहोविसृष्टं मिथुनीकृतस्य।
किं स्याच्चतुष्पात्प्रभवं च षड्भ्यो यत् स्त्रीषु गर्भत्वमुपैति पुंसः।। (च. शा.2/3)

When a woman after her menstruation cohabits with a man of a different clan in a lonely place, the man ejaculates *Shukra* (semen) which is implanted for the development of *Garbha* (embryo).

Even for procreation of a healthy child, it is necessary that both partners should be mutually from different clan. Coitus among the members of the same clan is said to be a sinful act. There are studies which help in proving this fact that chances of genetically carried diseases are more prone among such couples.

Marriage between blood relatives can lead to abnormal offspring due to genetic mismatch and hybrid DNA combinations. The *Gotra* system was defined around 4th century BCE to accommodate changed social rules and laws. With the passage of time, this system became an important parameter for finalizing a wedding, and is now a well-established system even in the modern society. Diseases like cystic fibrosis, phenylketonuria (PKU), galactosemia, retinoblastoma, albinism, sickle-cell anemia, thalassemia, Tay-Sachs disease, autism, growth hormone deficiency, adenosine deaminase deficiency, and juvenile muscular dystrophy are due to genetic disturbance.

Definition:

शुक्रशोणितजीवसंयोगे तु खलु कुक्षिगते गर्भसंज्ञा भवति।। (च. शा .4/5)

The union of *Shukra* (sperm), *Shonita (ovum)* and *Jeeva* (life) in the *Kukshi* (uterus) is known as *Garbha*.

Chakrapani says that in relation to development of *Garbha*, in one part of *Kukshi* (uterus), the *Aatma* always stay there.

Fig: 2.2.6 Stages from Ovulation to Implantation

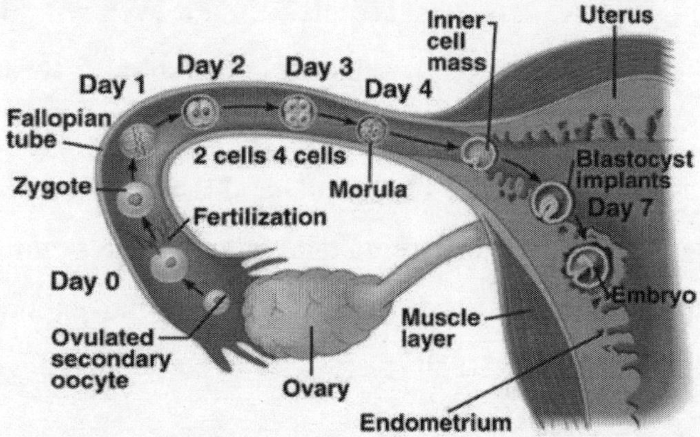

Fertilization takes place when one spermatozoon enters an ovum. The fused ovum and sperm forms the zygote. It takes place in the ampulla of the uterine tube. Further it goes under a series of division.

***Masa –Anumasik Vridhi* (Month Wise Fetal Development):**

The prenatal development of an individual is divided into **embryonic period** and **fetal period.** The embryonic developmental events can be studied according to days or weeks as per cited in modern textbooks of embryology.

In *Charaka Samhita,* the *Masa- Anumasik Vridhi* is the theory related to embryology. The month wise events are discussed occurring both in mother as well as fetus.

सर्वगुणवान् गर्भत्वमापन्नः प्रथमे मासि सम्मूर्च्छितः सर्वधातुकललीकृतः

खेटभूतो भवत्यव्यक्तविग्रहः सदसद्भूताङ्गावयवः।। (च.शा.4/9)

In the first month the embryo (awaited) having all qualities is in the form of *Kalal* (phlegm) with body parts being manifested or unmanifested.

According to modern science up to third month fetus growth is week wise. In first month the shape of fetus is *Kalala* and it is similar to morulla in modern science. During this month, it takes the form of jelly because of the intimate mixture of the five *Mahabhuta* and *Budbuda* stage similar to blastocyst.

द्वितीये मासि घनः सम्पद्यते पिण्डः पेश्यर्बुदं वा।

तत्र घनः पुरुषः, पेशी स्त्री, अर्बुदं नपुंसकम्।। (च.शा.4/10)

In second month development the phlegmatic compound solidified as a round structure indicating a *Purush* (male), elongated muscle type indicates *Stri* (female) and if it is similar to tumor then *Napunsaka* (eunuch) respectively.

The sex determination at this stage is quite difficult even with the modern techniques. The embryo growing in between 4th to 8th weeks becomes spirally twisted. Therefore limbs buds appear in the form of tubercles face completely develops, outer shape of the ear, nose and eyes become clearer. Blastula take the shape of gastrula and thus it is a three layered solid embryonic formative mass condensed with the differentiated cells of three germinal layers. These germinal layers are from outer to inner side, ectoderm, mesoderm and endoderm. As said by *Acharya Charaka*, at this stage (in third month) all sense organs, body parts develop.

The modern science states that in third month of intra uterine life, the size of the head becomes larger, whereas, the length of the neck increases. The limbs develop completely and nails of the digits also develop. External genitalia develop to such a degree that by the twelfth week the sex of the fetus can be determined by external examination. All the primary centers of the bony ossification develop in third month. Limbs (extremities) start develop in third month is similar to *Ayurveda* and modern science.

Bicardiac State:

According to *Ayurveda* the period of *Dauhradavastha* is a crucial period and begins at end of 3rd month up to starting of 4th month. Any disturbance during this period in the mother"s life may create developmental defects or malformations. It can be termed as a period of "congenital anomaly syndrome".

When *Indriya (*sense organs*)* are manifested in the *Garbha*, consciousness freely flows and then, there is *Spandan (*pulsation*)* in the *Garbha* and the desire for whatever was experienced in the previous life of individual. This condition is said to be *Dauhrda (*state of 2 hearts*)*. The heart of the *Garbha* is maternal in origin and is connected with the mother"s heart through the channels carrying nutrient material. There is exchange of feelings from each other. And this is the reason everybody should take care of it. If such desires are ignored, the *Garbha* may either be destroyed or get deformed. So it happens to be treating one and benefits are for both.

चतुर्थे मास स्थिरत्वमापद्यते गर्भः, ... । (च.शा.4/20)

During fourth month, the developing fetus gets more stable. According to modern science, the placental development is complete and the fetus becomes more constant.

Concept of Male or Female Child and Twin Pregnancy:

The vision of *Acharya Charaka* in context to *Linga Bedha* (sex determination) and twin pregnancy is benchmark in research. Without any technological hand he explained the concept regarding sex of fetus & twinning.

रक्तेन कन्यामधिकेन पुत्रं शुक्रेण तेन द्विविधीकृतेन।
बीजेन कन्यां च सुतं च सूते यथास्वबीजान्यतराधिकेन।।
शुक्राधिकं द्वैधमुपैति बीजं यस्याः सुतौ सा सहितौ प्रसूते।
रक्ताधिकं वा यदि भेदमेति द्विधा सुते सा सहिते प्रसूते।।
भिनत्ति यादव् बहुधा प्रपन्नः शुक्रार्तवं वायुरतिप्रवृद्धः।
तावन्त्यपत्यानि यथाविभागं कर्मात्मकान्यस्ववशात् प्रसूते।। (च.शा.2/12-14)

He elucidated the fact that due to dominance of *Shonita* (ovum) is more than the *Shukra* (sperm), it is a female child. But sperm dominance will produce a male child. Similarly, when the developed zygote splits into 2 parts and it has ovum dominancy, then female children or sperm dominant produces male children. The division is determined by the *Vayu* present and even due to past deeds.

In some case the fetus take a long time to develop due to poor nourishment and unhealthy condition of woman so fetus delivery is delayed.

So, this is the concept of *Acharya Charaka* regarding the sex determination and same in our modern science due to the content of sperm ovum, a sex of child is determined.

Sex Determination:

All ova contain 22+X chromosomes. The spermatozoa are of two types. Half of them have 22+X chromosomes and other have 22+Y chromosomes. They are called as gynosperms and androsperms.

These have "X-bearing" or "Y-bearing" spermatozoa. An ovum can be fertilized by either of the sperm (22+X or 22+Y). The zygote having 44+X+X chromosome gives girl as offspring. The zygote having 44+X+Y chromosome gives boy as offspring. Thus sex is determined at time of fertilization. Here "A" stands for autosomal chromosomes.

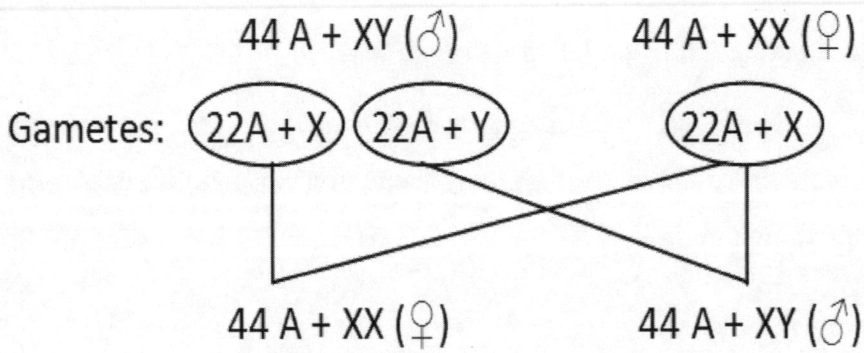

Fig: 2.7 Determination of Sex of the Fetus

In the associated context, multiple pregnancies mean that a woman has 2/more babies in her uterus. These can be from same egg or different (same-identical) or different (fraternal). Due to past deeds and uneven bifurcation of the zygote (from union of sperm- ovum) one in the twin pregnancy develops more and other is less developed.

Twin Pregnancy/ Multiple Pregnancies:

When a mother gives birth to two infants at the same time, they are called as twins. Three (triplets), four (quadruplets) are born simultaneously.

The process of hatching of blastocyst from zona pellucida may result in constriction of emerging cells and separation into 2 discrete entities. There is gradual decrease in average thickness of zona pellucida with increasing maternal age, which can be related to immune in frequency of monozygotic twinning with increased maternal age. The resultant twins have same genotype but differences in phenotypes.

Dizygotic Twins/ Fraternal:

Each developed from a separate ovum and separate spermatozoa. They have independent genetic constitution. They need not to be of same sex or they resemble each other.

Monozygotic:

The twins arise from single fertilized ovum. The genetic constitution of 2 twins is exactly the same. They have same sex.

Development of Twins:

The two twins do not undergo equal development, possibly as a result of unequal blood supply. The under developed fetus may possess no heart of its own and depend upon other fetus for its blood supply. It just sometimes represents just a mass attached to other fetus or embedded within its body.

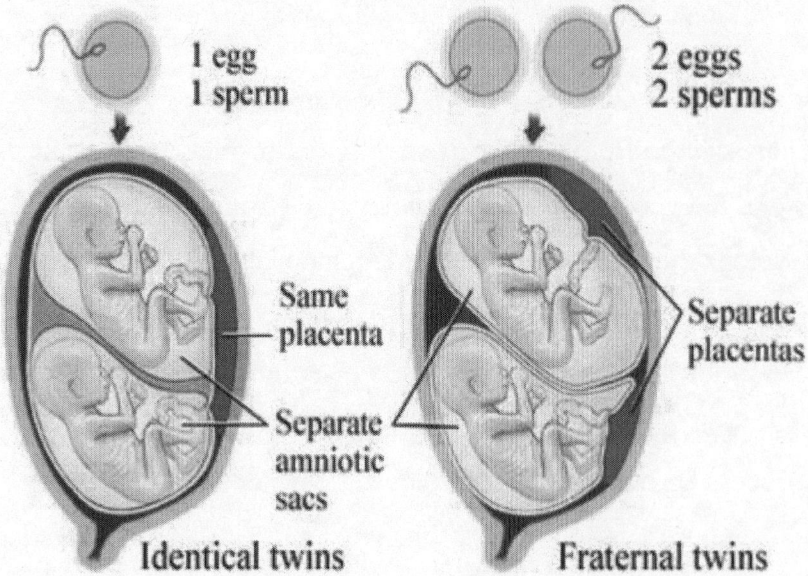

Fig: 2.8 Showing Twin Pregnancy

Factors responsible for abnormality in fetus:

The occurrence of sexual disorders is due to disturbance in the genetic composition.

बीजात् समांशदुपतप्तबीजात् स्त्रीपुंसलिङ्गी भवति द्विरेताः।
शुक्राशयं गर्भगतस्य हत्वा करोति वायुः पवनेन्द्रियत्वम्।।
शुक्राशयद्वारविघट्टनेन संस्कारवाहं कुरुतेऽनिलश्च।
मन्दाल्पबीजावबलावहर्षौ क्लीबौ च हेतुर्विकृतिद्वयस्य।।
मातुर्व्यवायप्रतिघेन वक्री स्याद् बीजदौर्बल्यतया पितुश्च।
ईर्ष्याभिभूतावपि मन्दहर्षौवीर्ष्यारतेरेव वदन्ति हेतुम्।। (च.शा .2/18-20)

When the developed zygote (union of sperm-ovum) is completely or partially damaged in terms of genetic portion, the progeny has characters of female and male *Dwireta* (hermaphrodite).

When due to *Vata*, the location of semen is disturbed it may result to *Pavanindriya* (devoid of semen). In the obstructed passage of semen, it causes *Klaibhya* (aphrodisiac). Due to damaged genetic portion and reduced reproductive factor results into male and female *Sandya* (sterility). Different types of factors are responsible for the origin to genetic sexual disorders. Improper hygiene of genitals, wrong position of coitus and lack of healthy gametes.

Describing abnormalities of sex in fetus causing impotency and explaining "*Dwireta*" is one of its types. *Acharya Chakrapani* says that the person affected has got the normal morphology of male and female in respect of common organs like eye, nose etc. but are devoid of specific sexual organs and secondary characters- breast, moustache, etc. the reason is that these organs and characters are caused by predominance of either male or female seed (sperm-ovum) but here both are in equal proportions.

Gene Abnormalities:

Genes are responsible for the normal embryological development. A change in the structure of a gene may occur at the time of gametogenesis. This may give rise to birth defects. The change in structure or function of a gene is called as gene mutation.

Hermaphroditism:

Abnormal development of gonad and the genitalia gives rise to various types of hermaphroditism. A hermaphrodite is in fact a person who is both a male, a female at same time. There are true hermaphrodites and pseudo hermaphrodites.

True Hermaphrodite:

The person has at least one testis, one ovary in body. The external genitalia may be male /female, midway between 2. The chromosomal sex may be either male or female.

False Hermaphrodite:

Gonads are of one sex while genitalia (internal/ external) are of opposite sex.

- Male hermaphrodite (testis)
- Female hermaphrodite (ovary)

Factors responsible for abnormality in fetus:

बीजात्मकर्माशयकालदोषैर्मातुस्तथाऽऽहारविहारदोषैः।
कुर्वन्ति दोषा विविधानि दुष्टाः संस्थानवर्णेन्द्रियवैकृतानि।।
वर्षासु काष्ठाश्मघनाम्बुवेगास्तरोः सरित्स्रोतसि संस्थितस्य।
यथैव कुयर्विकृतिं तथैव गर्भस्य कुक्षौ नियतस्य दोषाः।। (च.शा .2/29-30)

In answer to the question put up by *Agnivesha,* Lord *Atreya* replied that due to genetic factors, self deeds, by time period, mother"s food regime and behavioral activities; the vitiated *Dosha* result in many type of congenital abnormalities.

The concept of studying embryology is also important in studying the congenital abnormalities. If growing embryo is exposed to certain agents (chemical/physical) abnormalities in development can result. These agents are called as **"teratogens".** Teratological agents have greater impact on organ to organ.

Birth defect, congenital malformation, and congenital anomaly are synonymous terms used to describe structural, behavioral, functional, and metabolic disorders present at birth.

Malformations occur during formation of structures, for example, during organogenesis. They may result in complete or partial absence of a structure or in alterations of its normal configuration. The malformations are also caused by environmental or genetic factors acting independently or in concert. Most malformations have their origin during the third to eight weeks of gestation.

Congenital malformations in humans could also be caused by environmental factors like limb defects to the sedative **thalidomide** and it was clear that drugs could also cross the placenta and produce birth defects and many agents have been identified as **teratogens** (factors that cause birth defects).

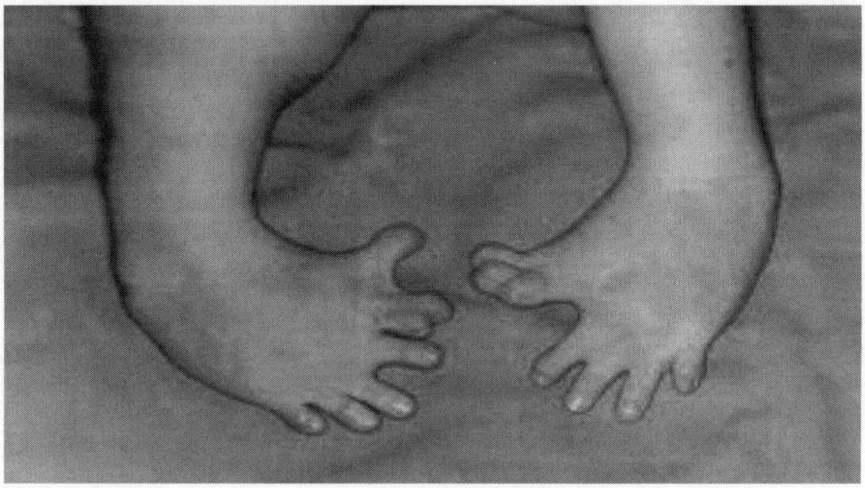

Fig: 2.9 Showing Thalidomide Effect on Limb

One of known social causes among birth defects are caused by the consumption of drugs such as LSD (lysergic acid diethylamide), PCP (phencyclidine,or "angel dust"), alcohol, smoking, cocaine etc.

There is a well- documented association between maternal alcohol ingestion and congenital abnormalities. Because alcohol may induce a broad spectrum of defects, ranging from intellectual disability to structural abnormalities of the brain (microcephaly, holoprosencephaly), face, and heart, the term **fetal alcohol spectrum disorder (FASD)** is used to refer to any alcohol-related defects. Cigarette smoking has been linked to an increased risk for orofacial clefts (cleft lip and cleft palate). It also contributes to intrauterine growth retardation and premature delivery.

So, from here the facts about *Anuvanshiki Sidhanata* and *Garbha Sharir* in *Ayurveda* are clear along with the contemporary science.

KEYS POINTS:

- The chapter concludes for the embryological, genetical facts mentioned by the *Acharya Charaka.*
- The concept of *Beeja* (Shukra –Shonita), *Beejabhaga* (chromosomal part) and *Beejabhagavayava* (genes).
- A number of chromosomal disorders, sex determination from both sciences have been included.
- Teratological impact due to external and internal environment has also been indicated by *Acharya.*

TWACHA SHARIR

(THE INTEGUMENTARY SYSTEM)

Introduction:

Twacha (skin) is the largest organ of the body and is of utmost importance as it decreases the socioeconomic status and affects the work ability of an individual. It is one of the five *Gyana Indriya* (sense organ) i.e. *Sparshgyana* (touch sensation) is received through it. The skin reflects the internal and external condition of body which helps in diagnosis of diseases.

Etymology:

In *Parishada Shabadartham*, the following synonyms are mentioned

चर्म, त्वक,त्वगिन्द्रिय, स्पर्शन,स्पर्शनेन्द्रिय

In the context of senses skin is the organ of touch "स्पर्शनेन्द्रिय (च.शा.1/30) "

The skin consists of epidermis, a superficial cellular layer and dermis and a deep connective tissue layer.

The skin is an interface with the environment; it plays a key immunity role in protecting the body against pathogens and excessive water loss. The other functions are insulation, temperature regulation, sensation, synthesis of vitamin D. In humans, skin pigmentation varies among populations and skin type from dry to oily. The actual skin color of different humans is affected by many substances, although the single most important substance determining human skin color is the pigment melanin. The pigment is produced by melanocytes.

***Twacha*:**

तमुवाच भगवानात्रेयः - श्रृणु मत्तोऽग्निवेश! सर्वशरीरमाचक्षाणस्य यथापश्नमेकमना यथावत्।
शरीरे षट् त्वचः; तद्यथा - उदकधरा त्वग्बाह्य, द्वितीया त्वसृग्धरा, तृतीया सिध्म-किलासम्भवाधिष्ठाना,
चतुर्थी दद्रुकुष्ठसम्भवाधिष्ठाना, पञ्चमी त्वलजीविद्रधिसम्भवाधिष्ठाना, षष्ठी तु यस्यां छिन्नायांताम्यत्यन्ध
इव च तमः प्रविशति यां चाप्यधिष्ठायारूंषि जायन्त, पर्वसु कृष्णरक्तानि स्थूलमूलानि
दुश्चिकित्स्यतमानि व इति षट् त्वचः। एताः षडङ्गंः शरीरमवतत्य तिष्ठन्ति ।। (च. शा.7/4)

There are six layers in the human body as answered by *Lord Atreya* to *Agnivesha* such as- the outermost is the *Udakadhara* (related to water content). The second layer is related to blood, third layer is said to be in relation to origin of *Sidhma* and *Kilasa* diseases, fourth layer has been associated with *Dadru* and *Kustha* . The fifth layer is seat of *Alaji* and *Vidradhi.* The sixth layer when gets injured, causes loss of consciousness and is the seat for origin to boils which are deep rooted on joints and hardly curable. Thus skin covers the entire body along with the six parts.

S.NO	LAYERS	DISEASES
1	*Udakdhara*	--------------
2	*Asrighdara*	--------------
3	*Triteeya*	*Sidhma, Switra*
4	*Chathurtha*	*Dadru,Kustha*
5	*Panchama*	*Alaji, Vidradhi*
6	*Sastha*	*Arsha , Bhagandara*

Table 3.1 Showing Layers of Skin with the Diseases

The third layer of skin is described as site of manifestation of *Sidhma* (type of dermatosis) and *Kilasa* (leucoderma). This layer of skin is actually the place where Doshas are vitiated to give rise to *Sidhma* and *Kilasa* are lodged.

Skin provides a uniquely accessible window for recognition of numerous and varied disorders. The clinical assessment of condition involving the patient's skin is the gross examination that is subsequently correlated with microscopic findings to make a diagnosis.

In general, it is composed of 2 layers, the epidermis and dermis separated by irregular border.

EPIDERMIS: It consists of following **5** layers.

1. **Basal Cell Layer [Stratum Germinatum]:**

The basal cell layer consists of a single layer of keratinocytes that forms the junction between the epidermis and dermis. The cells are interconnected with each other and with the overlying squamous cells by desmosomes. Interspersed in keratinocytes are melanocytes, a type of dendritic cells.

2. **Prickle Cell Layer[Stratum Spinosum, Stratum Malphighii]:**

It is composed of several layers of polygonal prickle cells or squamous cells. The layers become flat as they are near surface so that their long axis appears parallel to skin surface.

3. **Granular Cell Layer[Stratum Granulosum]:**

The layer consists of 1 to 3 layers of flat cells containing kerato- hyaline basophilic granules. These are thicker in palms and soles.

- Arrector pilori: small bundles of smooth muscles attached to hair follicle.(goose skin). They form diagonal links between the dermal sheaths of hair follicle and papillary layer of dermis.

- Nails:

  Thickening of deeper parts of stratum corneum, modified portion of skin called nail bed. They consist of compacted, anucleated, keratin-filled squames in two or three horizontal layers.

4. **Stratum Lucidum:**

This layer is also known as clear layer. It is present exclusively in palms-soles as a thin homogeneous, eosinophilic, non-nucleated zone. This layer presents a poorly understood stage in keratinocyte differentiation.

5. **Stratum Corneum [horny Layer]:**

The stratum corneum is also normally devoid of nuclei and consists of eosinophilic layers of keratin. Intra epidermal nerve endings are present in the form of merkel cells which are touch receptors.

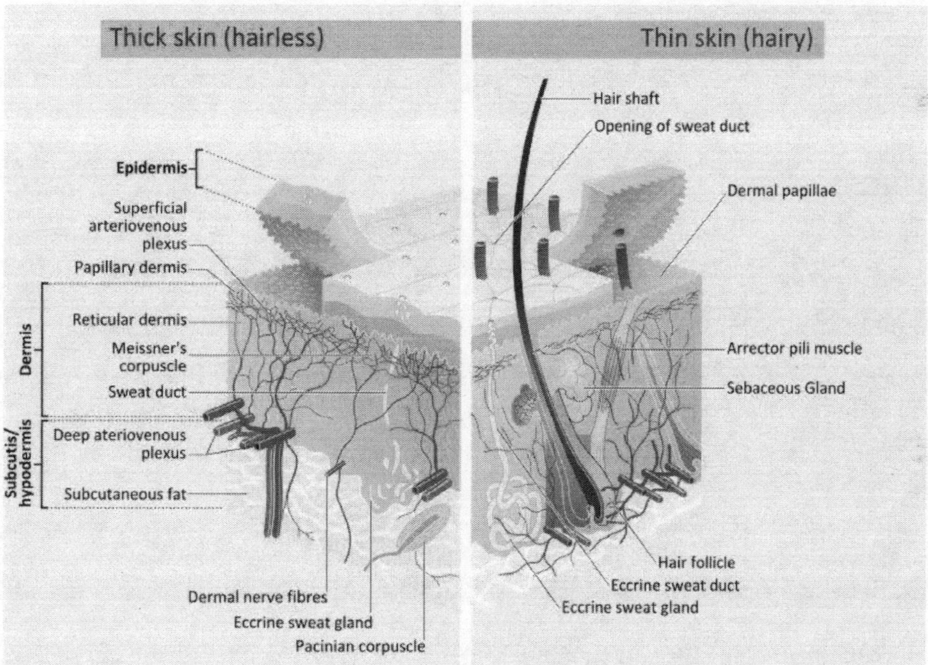

Fig: 3.1 Showing Features of Two Skin Type

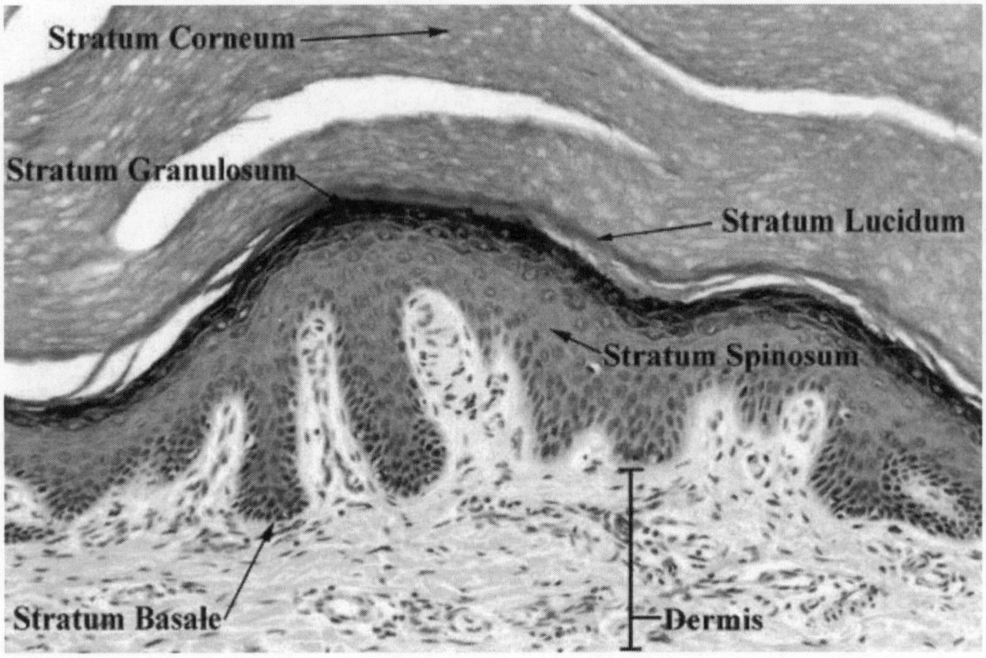

Fig: 3.2 Histological View to Epidermis

DERMIS:

It consists of 2 parts- superficial (pars papillaris) and deep part (pars reticularis). The dermis is composed of fibro collagen tissue containing blood vessels, lymphatics and nerves. The specialized nerve endings present at some sites perform specific functions.

1. Papillary layer:

It is immediately deep to epidermis and specialized to provide mechanical anchorage, metabolic support and maintenance to epidermis. The superficial surface of dermis is shaped into numerous papillae or rete ridges, which inter digitate with rete pegs in base of epidermis and form the dermo-epidermal junction at their interface. In thin skin, papillae are few, small at little mechanical stress and sensitive areas while thick skin of palm-sole the papillae are large and closely packed.

2. Reticular layer:

It merges with deep aspect of the papillary layer. The bundles of collagen fiber are thicker than those in papillary layer. The predominant orientation of the collagen fibers may be related to the local mechanical forces on dermis and thus involved in the development of skin lines.

Accessory features of skin:

- Pacinian corpuscles: concerned with pressure (deep layer)
- Meissner corpuscles: concerned with touch receptors
- Ruffini corpuscles and End bulb of Krause are the cold receptors of external genitalia.
- Sweat gland (Eccrine gland) present all over skin, but numerous on palms, soles, axillae; coiled tubular gland deep to dermis.
- Apocrine gland present in axillae , ano-genital , ceruminous glands.
- Sebaceous glands (holocrine) they are found everywhere on skin except on palms and soles.
- Hair: grows from bottom of follicle. It has intra cutaneous portion present in hair follicle and shaft.

Importance of Twacha Sharir:

वक्षयन्ते रक्तदोषजाः। कुष्ठवीसर्पपिडका रक्तपित्तमसृग्दरः।।
गुदमेढ्रास्यपाकश्च प्लीहा गुल्मोऽथ विद्रधिः। नीलिका कामला व्यङ्गः पिप्लत्तमसृग्दरः।।
दद्रुश्चर्मदलं श्वित्रं पामा कोठास्रमण्डलम्। रक्तप्रदोषाज्जायन्ते (च . सू. 28/11-12)

Many of the diseases Like *Kustha*, *Visarpa*, *Pidika*, *Asrigdara*, , *Guda-Medra Paka*, *Pleeha*, *Gulma*, *Kamala*, *Vyanga*, *Dadru*, *Charmadala*, *Shivitra* and other skin diseases are caused by morbidity of *Rakta Dhatu* . But all are observable through skin.[85]

According to *Acharya Chakrapani*, the reference of *Kustha* In *Rakta Dhatugata Roga* elucidates the other skin ailments like (*Dadru*). He also highlighted the fact that *Rakta Dosha* is the source of their origin.

In order to understand any skin disease (*Twacha Roga*) a detailed study of the structure and function of skin is necessary. The conceptual aspect of skin needs to be understood because skin disorder is outer exhibition of some kind of internal pathology. It is because skin is the most important factor involved in the pathogenesis of any disease which is manifested in the skin. *Twacha* is the most crucial site of expression and manifestation for most *Rogas*. Almost every *Roga* has its one or many *Lakshanas* having *Vyakti-Sthan* as *Twacha*.

Skin (*Twacha*) is one of the important presentable organ or the body. It has a definite role in one's personality. So, disorders of skin *(Twacha*) affect not only on somatic level but also on psychological level too.

DISEASES RELATED TO TWACHA SHARIR

KUSTHA :

The *Kustha Roga* has been portrayed in classical literature with very ideal observations. In *Shabada Kalpadrooma,* the term *"Kushnati"* is used for the abnormal condition (Structural change) of skin.

कुष्णाति शरीरस्थशोणितं विकुरूते इति ।। (श.क.द्रु.)

In *Ayurvedic* literature the description of *Kustha Roga* (like leprosy) is mentioned with the sign and symptoms. The basic clinical manifestations of *Kustha* are based on *Doshik* involvement like roughness, blue or bluish red color, dryness and pain, burning sensation, heaviness exudation etc. are due to *Tri Dosha* in all kinds of *Kustha.*

Suppression of sweating is considered to be a pre monitory symptom of *Kustha* due to vitiation of channels carrying sweat.

Different types of *Kustha* represent a mixture of signs and symptoms which are compared with the modern skin disorders especially with leprosy. Leprosy is considered to be more similar with the *Kustha Roga* as illustrated in *Ayurveda.*

Mahattva (greatness) of the *Kustha Roga* is due to quickly reaching the following *Dhatu*, its origin is from many *Doshik* constitution and from treatment point of view. *Acharya Chakrapani* says "severe pain" is one of their symptoms.

Prodormal Symptoms:

स्पर्शाज्ञत्वमतिस्वेदो न वा वैवर्ण्यमुन्नतिः। कोठानां लोमहर्षश्च कण्डूस्तोदः श्रमः क्लमः।।
व्रणानामधिकं शूलं शीघ्रोत्पत्तिश्चिरस्थितिः।। दाहः सुप्ताङ्गता चेति कुष्ठलक्षणमग्रजम् ।।
(च.चि.7/11-12)

As mentioned in the prodormal symptoms that loss of touch sensation, excessive or no perspiration, deranged complexion, appearance of rashes, horripilation, itching, piercing pain, excessive pain in wounds with origin and delayed healing and numbness in organs.

Chakrapani describes the *purvaroopa* (स्पर्शेत्यादि) and states that perspiration is affected by its absence or excessive presence. The lesion or wounds originate quickly and lasts for long time.

In this chapter, *Acharya Charaka* has mentioned 18 types of *Kustha.* The seven types of *Mahakustha* (major skin disorders or proper leprosy) are as- *Kapala Kustha, Audumbara, Mandala, Rsya-Jihva, Pundarika, Sidhma* and *Kakanaka Kustha* .

Along with this he has mentioned eighteen types of *Kshudra Kustha* (minor skin disorders). These are *Ekakustha, Charmakhya, Kitibha, Vipadika, Alasaka, Dadru, Charmadala, Pama, Visphota, Sataru* and *Vicarcika.* These are said to be curable as these are not deeply associated but *Maha Kustha* are mostly hard to cure or incurable.

S.No.	Name of *Kustha*	Possible Modern Correlation
1.	कपाल कुष्ठ	Non lepromatous leprosy
2.	उदुम्बर कुष्ठ	Non lepromatous leprosy
3.	मण्डल कुष्ठ	Lepromatous leprosy
4.	ऋष्यजिह्वा कुष्ठ	Non lepromatous leprosy
5.	पुण्डरीक कुष्ठ	Lepromatous leprosy
6.	सिध्मं कुष्ठ	Pityriasis versicolor
7.	काकणक कुष्ठ	Lepromatous leprosy
8.	एककुष्ठ कुष्ठ	Psoriasis
9.	चर्माख्य कुष्ठ	Psoriasis
10.	किटिभ कुष्ठ	Lichen planus
11.	वैपादिका कुष्ठ	Phagades
12.	अलसक कुष्ठ	-
13.	दद्रुमण्डल कुष्ठ	Ring worm
14.	चर्मदल कुष्ठ	Impetigo
15.	पामा कुष्ठ	Scabies
16.	विस्फोटक कुष्ठ	Exenthymeta
17.	शतारु कुष्ठ	Erythema induratum
18.	विचर्चिका कुष्ठ	Eczema

Table: 3.2 Showing Different *Kustha Roga* with Modern Correlation

Leprosy:

It is a chronic non fatal infectious disease affecting mainly the cooler parts of the body such as skin, mouth respiratory tract, eyes, peripheral nerves, superficial lymph nodes and testis.

- Tuberculoid leprosy:

The skin lesions are asymmetrical, single or a few lesions, hypo-pigmented and erythmatous macular.

The nerve involvement is present with distinct sensory disturbances.The histopathology aspects hard tubercle similar to granulomatous lesion, eroding the basal layer of epidermis, no clear zone.

Bacteriology- *Leprae bacilli* few, seen in destroyed nerves as granular or beaded forms. There is distinct sensory impairment. Lesion of tuberculoid leprosy have predilection for dermal nerves which may be destroyed, in filtered by epitheloid cells and lymphocytes.

Clinical studies use the Ridley-Jopling system. It has six classifications based on severity of symptoms. They are:

S.No	Type of Leprosy	Clinical Features
1.	Inter mediate leprosy	A few flat lesions heal by self or can progress to severity.
2.	Tuberculoid leprosy	Flat lesion, large, numbness, nerve involvement
3.	Borderline leprosy	Similar to tuberculoid, small-numerous lesions, less nerve entrapment
4.	Mid- borderline leprosy	Reddish plaques, numbness, lymph glands swollen.
5.	Borderline lepromatous leprosy	Many flat lesion, raised bumps, nodules, sometimes numbess
6.	Lepromatous leprosy	Lesions with bacteria, hair loss, nerve involvement, weakness, disfigurement

Table: 3.3 Showing Classification of Leprosy

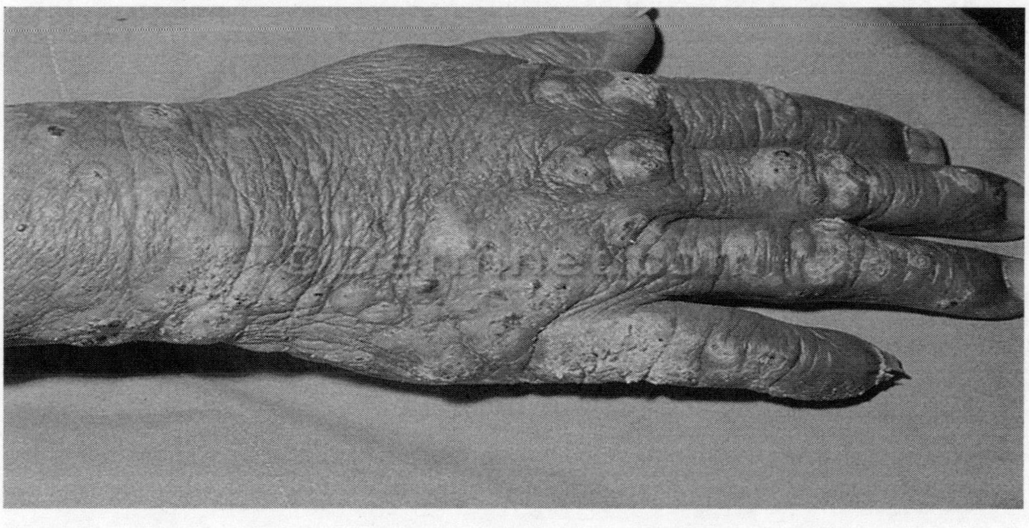

Fig: 3.3 Affected Limb Due To Leprosy

EKA KUSTHA:

अस्वेदनं महावास्तु यन्मत्स्यशकलोपमम्।   (च.चि.7/21)

The clinical feature in *Eka Kustha* refers to absence of perspiration (*Aswedanm*), skin peels or looks like scaly skin of fish. These features can be compared with clinical presentation of a psoriatic patient.

Chakrapani explains that the disease spreading over a large area of body. The appearance of skin resembles with fish skin. He also adds that the skin becomes coarse and uneven due to presence of lesions/ wounds.

Psoriasis: The chronic inflammatory dermatosis.

Morphology:

There is marked epidermal thickening [acnathosis], with regular downward elongation of rete ridges. Increased epidermal cell turnover and lack of maturation result in loss of stratum granulosum with extensive overlying para keratotic scale.

There is thinning of epidermal cells layer overlying tips of dermal papillae and blood vessels within papillae are dilated and tortuous. These vessels bleed readily when scale is removed [Auspitz sign].

Clinical features:

It affects skin of elbows, knees, scalp, lumbosacral areas, inter gluteal cleft, glans penis. The most typical lesion is a well demarcated, pink to salmon colored plaque covered by loosely adherent silver white scale.

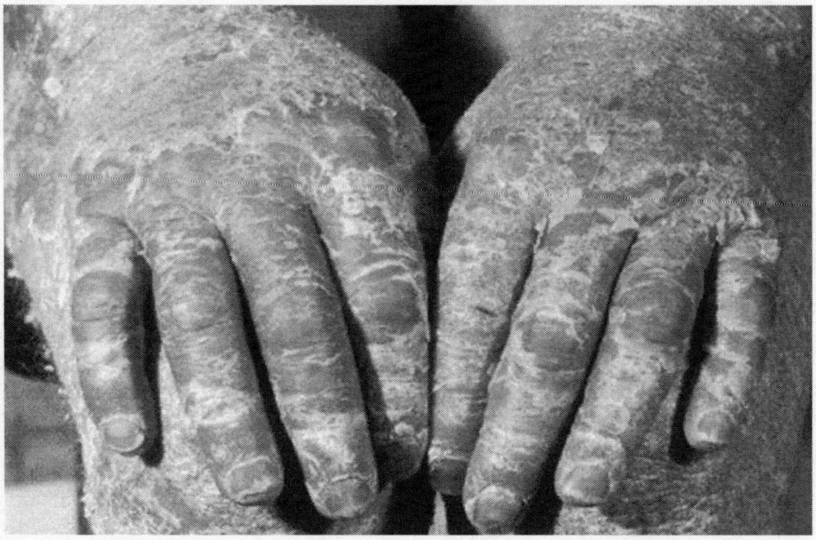

Fig: 3.4 Epidermal Thickening in Psoriasis

तदेककुष्ठं - चर्माख्यं बहलं हस्तिचर्मवत्।। (च.चि.7/21)

Even in *Charmakhya Kustha* the skin becomes thick-skinned like elephant. Most of the features are similar to that of psoriasis.

VICHARCHIKA :

रक्तं श्यावं सदाहार्तिं शतारुः स्याद् बहुव्रणम्।
सकण्डूः पिडका श्यावा बहुस्रावा विचर्चिका।। (च.चि.7/26)

In case of *Vicharchika,* presence of red, blackish coloured *Vrana* (pimples) along with pain and burning sensation. There is itching, oozing *Vrana* are present. Such types of features we find in a patient suffering from eczema. So the features mentioned in the context are correlated to eczema.

Eczema:

It is a clinical term that embraces a number of conditions with different etiologies. They are characterized by red, papulo-vesicular, and oozing, crusted lesions at an early stage. The lesions develop into raised, scaling plaques.

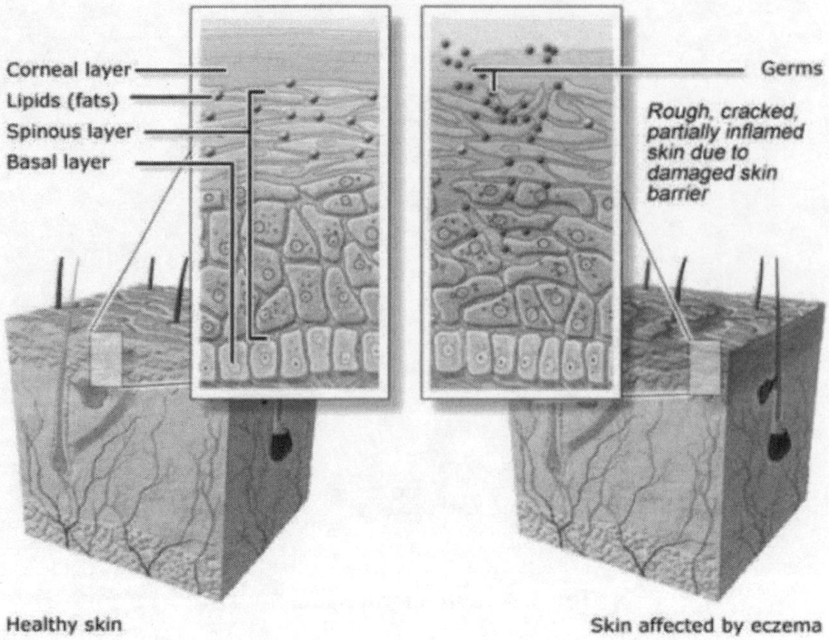

Fig: 3.5 Comparison of the Normal Skin with Eczema

Morphology:

The accumulation of edema fluid within the epidermis characterizes all forms of acute eczematous dermatitis (spongiotic dermatitis). Edema develops into intercellular spaces of epidermis, splaying apart keratinocytes. A superficial perivascular lymphocytic infiltrate, papillary dermal edema, mast cell degranulation.

Clinical features:

Lesions are pruritic (itchy), edematous, oozing plaques, vesicles and bullae.

Chronic dermatitis:

It shows hyper keratosis, parakeratosis, acanthosis with elongation of rete ridges and broadened dermal papillae.

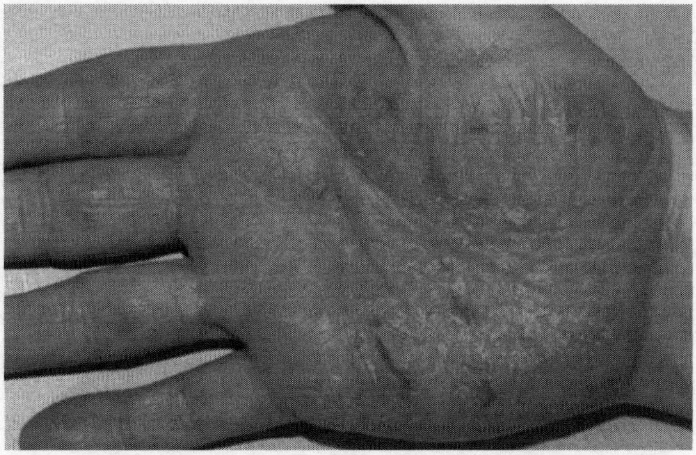

Fig: 3.6 Showing Eczematous Hand

CHARMADALA

रक्तं सकण्डु सस्फोटं सरुग्दलति चापि यत्।
तच्चर्मदलमाख्यातं संस्पर्शासहमुच्यते।। (च.चि.7/24)

In this type of *Kustha* presence of red, associated with itching, eruptions and pain, leaves off flakes and has tenderness. The sign and symptom refers with the condition of impetigo.

Impetigo:

Impetigo is a common superficial bacterial infection caused by staphylococci and streptococci.

Histological, characteristic feature is sub corneal pustule which is a collection of neutrophils under stratum corneum. A few acantholytic cells and gram +ve bacteria are found within pustule. The upper dermis contains severe inflammatory reaction composesd of neutrophils, lymphoids cells.

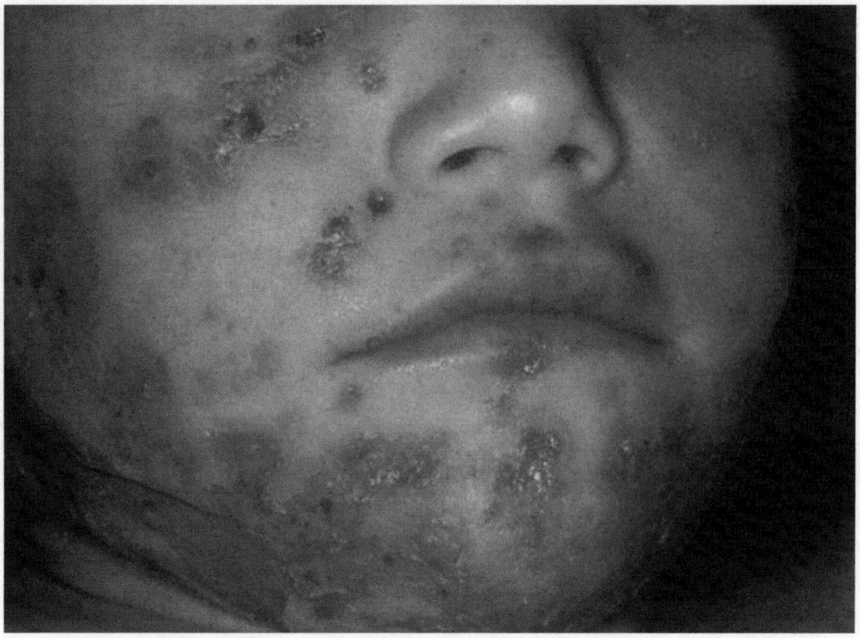

Fig: 3.7 Clinical Feature of Impetigo

KITIBAH

श्यावं किरणखरस्पर्शं परुषं किटिभं मतम्।
वैपादिकं पाणिपादस्फुटनं तीव्रवेदनम्।। (च.चि.7/22)

Kitibah Kustha represents with blackish, rough like a corn and coarse. The skin texture changes to roughness. The sign and symptoms relate to condition of lichen planus.

Lichen Planus:

Lichen planus is a chronic dermatosis characterized clinically by irregular, violaceous, shining, flat topped, pruritic papules. The lesions are distributed symmetrically with sites of predilection being flexor surfaces of the wrists, forearms, legs and external genitalia. Buccal mucosa is also involved in many cases of lichen planus. Histologically, the characteristic features are as:

i) Marked hyperkeratosis.
ii) Focal hypergranulosis.
iii) Irregular acanthosis with elongated saw-toothed rete ridges.
iv) Liquefactive degeneration of the basal layer.

v) A band-like dermal infiltrate of mononuclear cells, sharply demarcated at its lower border and closely joined with the basal layer.

SLIPADA:

जङ्घासु पिण्डीप्रपदोपरिष्टात् स्याच्छ्लीपदं मांसकफास्रदोषात्।
सिराकफघ्नश्च विधिः समग्रस्तत्रेष्यते सर्षपलेपनं च।। (च.चि.12/97)

Due to vitiation of *Mamsa, Kapha* and *Rakta* there is swelling in the shank region from feet to calf muscles. It is known as *Slipada* (filaria) and there is venous congestion which must be removed.

Acharya Chakrapani says that the swelling persisting in *Slipada roga* is not limited to one region of body however it may involve other regions of the body.

Slipada can be correlated with the Filariasis/elephantiasis disease. The sign and symptoms are similar to each other.

The Anatomy of Lymphatic System:

The fluid during circulation enters a separate system of lymphatic vessels (lymphatic). The fluid passing through these vessels is called as lymph.

The components are: lymphatic plexuses, a network of lymphatic capillaries. The smallest lymph vessels are lymphatic capillaries that join together to form larger lymphatic vessels. The largest lymphatic vessel present in the body is thoracic duct.

Along the vessels there are numerous small bean shaped structures called lymph nodes (present in groups). These are masses of lymphoid tissue. These nodes act as filters removing bacteria and other particulate matter from lymph. The lymphoid organs are thymus, red bone marrow, spleen, tonsils, solitary, aggregated lymphoid nodules (alimentary tract, appendix).

Lymphatic Obstruction:

Normally, the interstitial fluid in the tissue spaces escapes by way of lymphatics. Obstruction to outflow of these channels causes localized edema, known as lymph edema. Inflammation of the lymphatic's as seen in filariasis (infection with Wuchereria bancrofti) results in chronic lymph edema of scrotum and legs known as "elephantiasis".

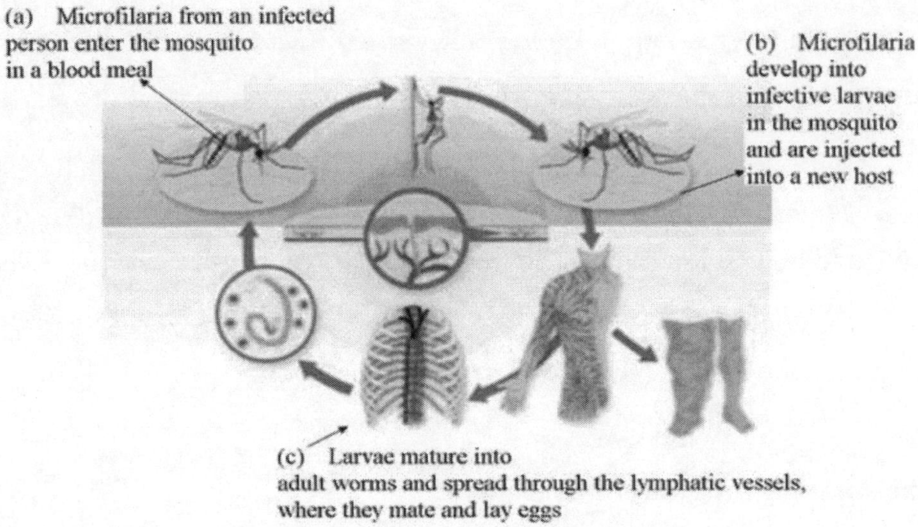

Fig: 3.8 Pathogenesis of Filaria

Filariasis:

Wuchereria bancrofti and *Brugia malayi* are responsible for causing Bancroftian and Malayan filariasis in different geographic regions. The lymphatic vessels inhabit the adult worm, especially in the lymph nodes, testis and epididymis. Microfilariae seen in the circulation are produced by the female worm .Majority of infected patients remain asymptomatic. Symptomatic cases may have two forms of disease—an acute form and a chronic form.

Acute form of filariasis presents with fever, lymphangitis, lymphadenitis, epididymo-orchitis, urticaria, eosinophilia and microfilariaemia.

Chronic form of filariasis is characterized by lymphadenopathy, lymph edema, hydrocele and elephantiasis.

Morphologic Features:

The most significant histological changes are due to the presence of adult worms in the lymphatic vessels causing lymphatic obstruction and lymphoedema. The regional lymph nodes are enlarged and their sinuses are distended with lymph. The tissues surrounding the blocked lymphatics are infiltrated by chronic inflammatory cell infiltrate consisting of lymphocytes, histiocytes, plasma cells and eosinophils. Chronicity of the process causes enormous thickening and indurations of the skin of legs and scrotum resembling the hide of an elephant and hence the name elephantiasis.

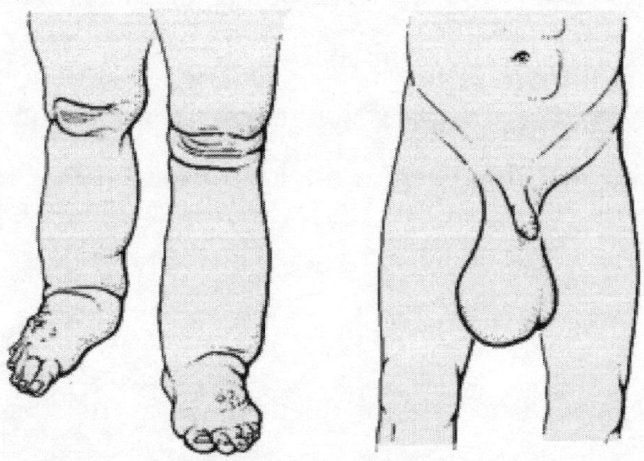

Fig: 3.9 Showing Hydrocele and Swollen Limb

KAMALA :

हारिद्रनेत्रः स भृशं हारिद्रत्वङ्नखाननः। रक्तपीतशकृन्मूत्रो भेकवर्णो हतेन्द्रियः।।
दाहाविपाकदौर्बल्यसदनारुचिकर्षितः। कामला बहुपित्तैषा कोष्ठशाखाश्रया मता।।
(च.चि.16/35-36)

There are following signs and symptoms in a patient of *Pandu Roga* when not treated properly. The patient's eyes, nails, skin and face become deep yellow; faeces and urine turns as red and yellow. The senses and organs lose their functions and he suffers from burning sensation, indigestion, debility, malaise and anorexia. The passage of *kamala* (jaundice) is said to be in *Kostha* (belly region) and *Shakha* (Twach, Rakta etc) along with the vitiation of *Pitta* and *Rakta.*

The concept of *Kamala* whether *Kosthagata* or *Shakhagata* have features similar to jaundice. The types of jaundice can be compared with the types of *Kamala* as both have same clinical features observed in the patients.

Normal Anatomy of Biliary Ducts and Gall Bladder

The biliary ducts convey bile from the liver to duodenum. It is produced by the liver and stored and concentrated in gall bladder. Normal hepatic tissue, demonstrated as hexagonal shaped liver lobule. Each lobule has a central vein running through center from which sinusoids (large capillaries) and plates of hepatocytes (liver cells) radiate toward an imaginary perimeter extrapolated from surrounding interlobular portal triads (terminal branches of the hepatic portal vein and artery and initial branches of biliary ducts).

The bile duct (called as common bile duct) is formed by the union of cystic duct and common hepatic duct. The gall bladder lies in the fossa for the gall bladder on the visceral surface of the liver.

Applied Anatomy:

In certain liver disorders, a yellow pigment called bilirubin builds up in the blood, giving a yellow appearance to white of eyes, skin, a condition called jaundice.

Jaundice refers to a yellowish tint to the body tissues, including a yellowness of the skin and deep tissues. The usual cause of jaundice is large quantities of bilirubin in the extracellular fluids, either un-conjugated or conjugated bilirubin. The skin usually begins to appear jaundiced when the concentration rises to about three time normal-that is, above 1.5 mg/dl.

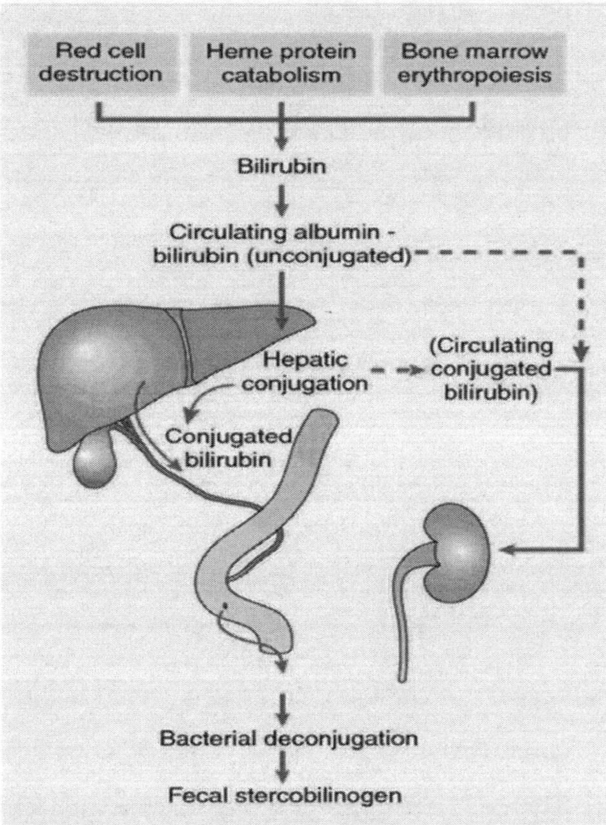

Fig.2.3.10 Showing the Normal Bilirubin Circulation

These two types of jaundice are called, respectively, hemolytic jaundice and obstructive jaundice. They differ from each other in the following ways. Hemolytic jaundice is caused by hemolysis of red blood cells and obstructive jaundice is caused by obstruction of bile ducts or liver disease.

In obstructive jaundice, caused either by obstruction of the bile ducts (which most often occurs when a gallstone or cancer blocks the common bile duct) or by damage to the hepatic cells (which occurs in hepatitis), the rate of bilirubin formation is normal, but the bilirubin formed cannot pass from the blood into the intestines. The unconjugated bilirubin still enters the liver cells and becomes conjugated in the usual way. This conjugated bilirubin is then returned to the blood, probably by rupture of the congested bile canaliculi and direct emptying of the bile into the lymph leaving the liver. Thus, most of the bilirubin in the plasma becomes the conjugated type rather than the unconjugated type.

A gall stone is a concretion in the gall bladder, cystic duct or bile duct composed chiefly of cholesterol crystals. For any clinical relevance, they must obtain a size sufficient to produce mechanical injury to the gall bladder or obstruction of the biliary tracts.

KEYS POINTS:

- The skin is reflection of our internal health status, so it is vital to take care of it.
- The chapter highlights the surface anatomy and histological view of afflicted skin, which is essential for examination of a patient.
- Diseases like various *Kustha* (related with Leprosy), *Slipada* (filiarisis), *Kamala* (jaundice) has been included.

REVIEW ON UTTAMANGIYA SHARIR

(THE NERVOUS SYSTEM)

Introduction:

In *Ayurvedic* science, the *Trimarma* (vital parts) are considered important due to residence of *Prana* (life). Their consideration is important in building up the body's framework and its destruction leads to serious disruption of life. It is not only important in carrying life processes but management is also required on occurrence of serious diseases.

In this chapter, the emphasis has been laid on *Shira*, *Urdhva- Jatrugata Roga* and *Sarvanga Sharir.* The diseases mentioned here are mostly due to affliction of *Vata Dosha* along with other *Dosha.*

Etymology:

- The word *Shira* is derived from (शृ) *Dhatu* and(असुन्) Pratya,

  शृ + असुन् प्रत्यय।। (वा.)

- In *Shabada Kalpadrooma, Shira* is specified as,

  श्रि + श्रयते: स्वाङ्गे शिर: किच्च् । शिर: कपालोऽस्यातीति इति:।।

  मूर्धा मूर्धा शिरो देशे पुंसि स्यातामिमौ समौ ।। (श.क.द्रु. भाग 5)

- Sir Monier Williams dictionary it is enumerated as,

  शिर: शूलं- शिरस: शूलम्। मस्तक वेदनारोग:।।

उत्तमाङ्ग के पर्याय (Synonyms):

उत्तमाङ्ग, शिर ,मस्तक ,चेत:, चेतना स्थान ,मूर्धा ,कपाल

The word used for *Shira* (head) and *Shirogriva* (head neck). In reference to the term **चेतः, चेतना स्थान** , is used as carrier of senses and for *Mana. Acharya Chakrapani* says it as *Mastishka, Murdha* (on injury leads to fatal condition).

SIGNIFICANCE OF SHIRA:

प्राणाः प्राणभूतां यत्र श्रिताः सर्वेन्द्रियाणि च।
यदुत्तमाङ्गमङ्गानां शिरस्तदभिधीयते।। (च.सू.17/12)

The *Shira* (head) is important organ where all sense organs and their receptors reside. In the reference to the head diseases, *Acharya Charaka* has mentioned *Shira* (head) among one of the site of *Prana* (vital breath) in living body.

Acharya Chakrapani says that *Shira* (head) is well thought-out as superior among organs. Any type of injury can lead to severe outcomes and death can occur. He told that *Prana* and *Indriyas* (sense organs) dwell here and is higher organ of body.

In *Charaka Pradipika*, it is acknowledged that *Shira* (head) is the site for all sense organs. On any damage or affliction, the sense organs lose their ability and thus it seems to be true (head as important).

In modern science, Brain is considered to be one of the organs among the **"tripod of life"** and even associated region like carotid or neck region can also lead to symptoms of fatality.

Similarly, this chapter constitutes those diseases where one can find a relative correlation to disorders confined to nervous system. Due to affliction of *Vata Dosha* the various symptoms are produced in different region of the body. The nervous system is chief controller and coordinator of all activities in body. The system has a control over all parts of the body through its supply.

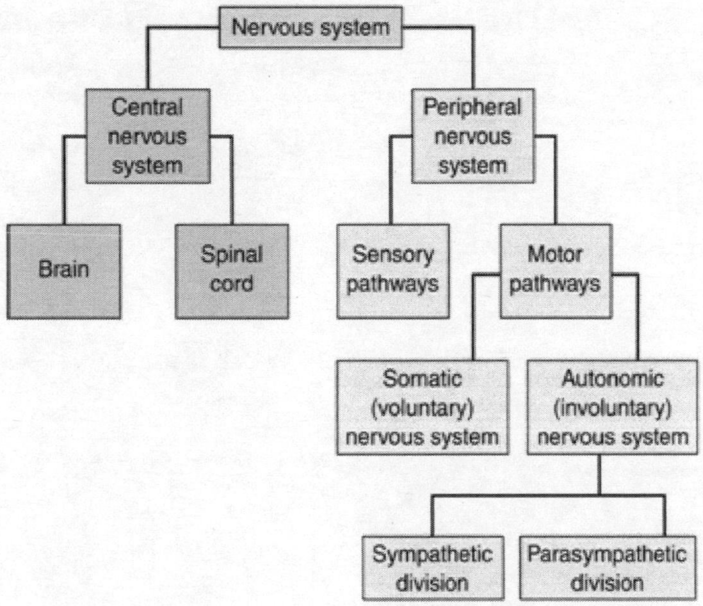

Fig. 4.1 Showing the Divisions of Nervous System

In *Ayurveda Vata* (as *Dosha*) & *Vayu* (as *Panchamahabhuta*) are the dominating factors for *Gati* (movement), receiving impulses. It is similar to the nervous system of contemporary science exhibiting the same functional properties. The functions of *Vata* are not limited but inevitable for systemic activity.

Shira as Sthana* of *Prana:

दशैवायतनान्याहुः प्राणा येषु प्रतिष्ठिताः।
शङ्खौ मर्मत्रयं कण्ठो रक्तं शुक्रौजसी गुदम्।। (च.सू.29/3)

Among the ten *Pranayatna* (vital sites) stated by *Acharya Charaka shira* (head region) has been given prime importance. Along with other parts, *Shira* also has its own importance in maintaining life. So a wise physician should always know their importance while treatment procedures and in maintaining a healthy life. Everything we do or say depends on our brain activities. The brain is divided into region which controls various functions such as movement, speech, balance. Damage to a region may affect the function it controls, causing symptom such as loss of movement, difficulty speaking or loss of consciousness.

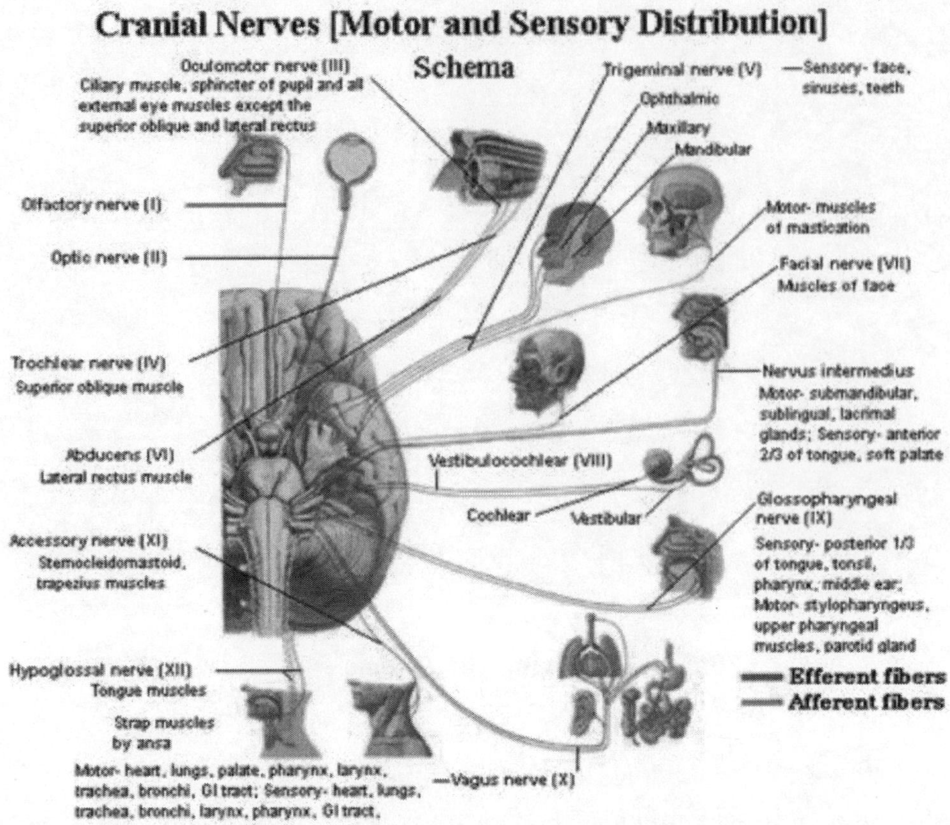

Fig: 4.2 Illustrating Motor & Sensory Supply from Brain

शिरसी इन्द्रियाणि इन्द्रिय प्राणवहानि च।
श्रोतांसि सूर्यमिव गभस्तय: संश्रितानि ।। (च .सि.9/4)

All sense organs and the channels carrying the sensory and vital impulses from the *Shira* are like the rays from the sun. The quotation affirmed truly signifies *Shira* as a *Trimarma* as it correlates it completely to the brain. Thus, even if there is any minor injury to the organ leads to death or disastrous symptoms.

***Shira* as *Marma*:**

- म+ सर्व धातुभ्यो मनिन् ।। (श.क.द्रु. भाग 3)

The word "*Marma*" (vital point) states a site, where due to any injury the signs and symptoms are more towards the disability or death.

- मृ - मनिन् -जीवस्थाने् , सन्धिस्थाने, तातपर्ये च।।

In *Shabdastoma*, it is derived from (मृ) *Dhatu* and (मनिन्) *Pratya* & is known as *Jeevasthana* & *Sandhisthana*.

Acharya Charaka stated in one of the reference that *Marmas* are those points where pain is felt more intensively than any other region. From this reference we can state that head is one of crucial organ of the body to which any injury occurs and it will be fatal.

***Marma Aaghat Lakshan*:**

..... शिरस्यभिहते मन्यास्तम्भार्दितचक्षुर्विभ्रममोहोद्वेष्टनचेष्टानाशकास श्वासहनुग्रह मूकगद्गदत्वाक्षिनि मीलनगण्डस्पन्दनजृम्भणलालास्रावस्वरहानिवदनजिह्मत्वादीनि; । (च. सि.9/6)

Whenever any *Marma* point is injured, its consequences are fatal for life. The *Shira* (head) is crucial organ and when it is affected then there is stiffness in the carotid region, facial paralysis, rolling of eye balls, confusion (mental), cramps, loss of movement, cough, dyspnoea, lock-jaw, stammering, ptosis, yawning, loss of voice and crooked face etc. Due to any trauma over head or nearby region (neck) major functions, control and coordination gets disturbed.

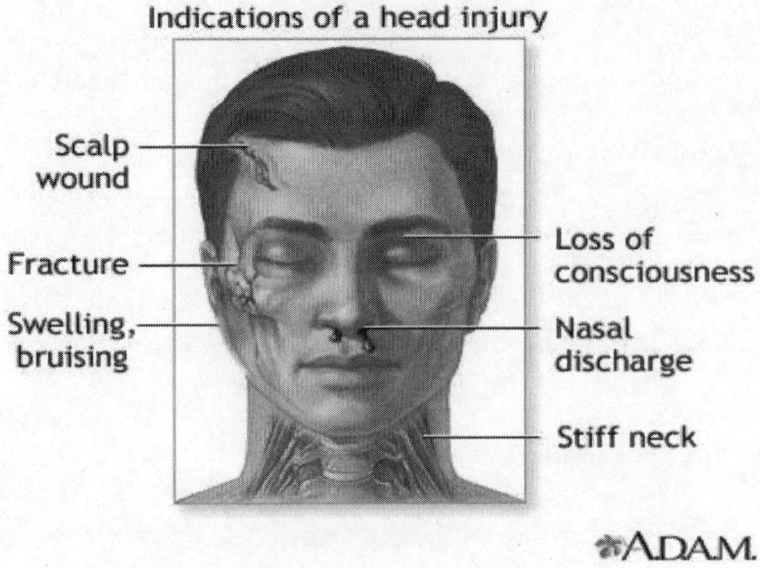

Fig: 4.3 Indications of Head Injury

DISEASES RELATED TO UTTAMANGIYA SHARIR

Following are the diseases mentioned in this chapter with their possible association in modern medical science.

ARDITA:

अतिवृद्धः शरीरार्धमेकं वायुः पपद्यते। यदा तदोपशोष्यासृग्बाहुं पादं च जानु च।।
तस्मिन् सङ्कोचयत्यर्ध मुखं जिह्मं करोति च। वक्रीकरोति नासाभ्रूललाटाक्षिहनूस्तथा।।
ततो वक्रं व्रजत्यास्ये भोजनं वक्रनासिकम्। स्तब्धं नेत्रं कथयतः क्षवथुश्च निगृह्यते।।दीना जिह्म
समुत्क्षिप्ता कला सज्जति चास्य वाक्।दन्ताश्चलन्ति बाध्येते श्रवणौ भिद्यते स्वरः।।
पादहस्ताक्षिजङ्गोरुशङ्खश्रवणगण्डरुक्। अर्धे तस्मिन्मुखार्धे वा केवले स्यात्तदर्दितम्।।
(च.चि.28/38-42)

In the chapter titled "*Vata Vyadhi*" *Acharya* has mentioned *Ardita Roga*. The provoked *Vata* affects one side of body, it dries up blood, hand, leg, and knee and there is contraction of the side. Along with this, eye, nose, eyebrows, jaws gets crooked. Thus, the opening of the mouth goes in crooked manner, difficulty in having food, tongue becomes curved when raised, nose gets deviated, and hearing and speech is affected. The disease is diagnosed with the one-sided or half side of the body.

Chakrapani elucidated *Ardita Roga* with his words that aggravated *Vayu* affects one side of body. He also highlighted indistinct voice and hearing ability is also affected of the patient.

The correlation of *Ardita Roga is* made with the facial paralysis caused by seventh cranial nerve. The detail of the nerve is mentioned here along with the clinical aspect in diagnosing facial paralysis.

Anatomy of Facial Nerve:

The facial nerve emerges from base of skull at stylo-mastoid foramen. It gains access to face while passing from the parotid gland. Near this foramen the nerve gives a posterior auricular nerve and within the substance of gland it divides into temporo-facial and cervico-facial trunks. The trunk further forms a plexuses and gives five branches. [124]

- ✓ Temporal branch
- ✓ Zygomatic branch
- ✓ Buccal branch
- ✓ Mandibular branch
- ✓ Cervical branch

The facial nerve is a mixed type of nerve and its innervations are as follows enlisted in the table.

Sensory Root	Motor Root	Parasympathetic Root
Innervation for taste sensation	Somatic innervations	Secretions of glands Lacrimal, sublingual, submandibular

Table: 4.1 Enlisting the Facial Nerve Innervation

Facial paralysis:

Facial nerve paralysis may be due to an upper motor neuron lesion, or a lower motor neuron lesion. Bell's palsy and acoustic neuromas can produce a complete lower motor neuron facial paralysis.

Facial nerve is the most frequently paralyzed cranial nerve. Depending on location of lesion different symptoms occur. A lesion of CN VII near its origin, or geniculate ganglion will accompanied by loss of motor, gustatory (taste) and autonomic function.

A central lesion results in paralysis of muscles in the inferior face on contra lateral side. Bell's palsy is unilateral facial paralysis of sudden onset resulting from lesion.[126]

In Bell's palsy facial muscles get paralyzed on affected side, facial expression is distorted, loss of tonus of orbicularis oculi causes inferior eyelid to evert. When buccinators or orbicularis oris is affected the food will accumulate in oral cavity. When sphincters of mouth are affected, displacement of mouth (drooping of corners) is produced. Weakened lip muscles affect speech also.

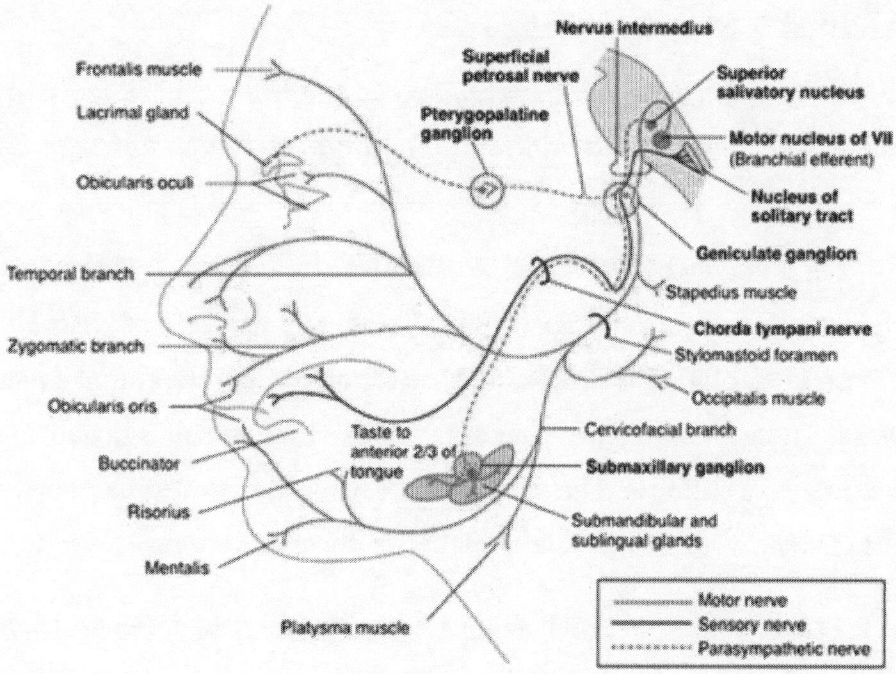

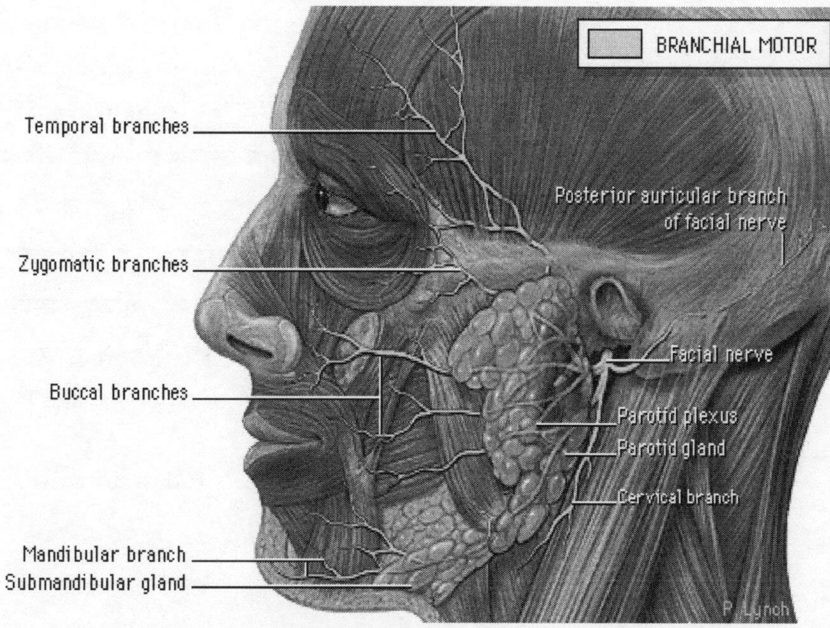

Fig: 4.4 Course and Branches of Facial Nerve

AKESHAPA AND DANDAKA:

महुराक्षिपति क्रुद्धो गात्राण्याक्षेपकोऽनिलः।। पाणिपादं च संशोष्य सिराः सस्नायुकण्डराः।
पाणिपादशिरः पृष्ठश्रोणीः स्तभ्नानि मारुतः।।दण्डवत्स्तब्धगात्रस्य दण्डक :। (च.चि.28/50-51)

In *Vata Vyadhi* chapter he has given reference of symptoms which affect the different parts of the body in various forms. The affliction due to *vata dosha* results in stiffness of carotid region, neck, and salivation occurs, back turns inward and lock-jaw is present. The *vata* on aggravation dries up external vessels situated in back, carotids and cause arc- like stiffness. The patients back bends downward like bow, head goes to back, chest gets thrown upwards, and neck bends downwards.

There is loss of speech and patient puts a force to speak which makes him restless. The presence of convulsion in the body results in drying of hands-feet along with blood vessels, ligament and tendon. This condition refers to *akeshapa.* And when there is stiffness occurs in hands, feet, head, back, hip like a stick it is known as *dandaka*.

मन्ये संश्रित्य वातोऽन्तर्यदा नाडीः प्रपद्यते। मन्यास्तम्भं तदा कुर्यादन्तरायामसंज्ञितम्।।
अन्तरायम्यते ग्रीवा मन्या च स्तभ्यते भृशम्। दन्तानां दंशनं लाला पृष्ठाक्षेपः शिरोग्रहः।।
जृम्भा वदनसङ्गश्चाप्यन्तरायामलक्षणम्। इत्युक्तस्त्वन्तरायाम :- - बहिरायाम उच्यते।।
पृष्ठमन्याश्रिता बाह्याः शोषयित्वा सिरा बली। वायुः कुर्याद्धनुस्तम्भं बहिरायामसंज्ञकम्।।
चापवन्नाम्यमानस्य पृष्ठतो नीयते शिरः। उर उत्क्षिप्यते मन्या स्तब्धा ग्रीवाऽवमृद्यते।।
दन्तानां दंशनं जृम्भा लालास्रवाश्च वाग्ग्रहः। जातवेगो निहन्त्येष वैकल्यं वा प्रयच्छति।
(च .चि.28/43-48)

Even *Chakrapani* states the same condition but with difference in phrases, all the symptoms like stiffness in sterno-mastoid region, clenching of teeth, excessive salivation, rigidity in head and face region.

The above mentioned conditions are related with each other. In opisthotonus there is severe hyper extension and spasticity in which an individual's head neck and spinal column enter into a complete bridging or "arching" position. It can be caused due to intoxication, strychnine poisoning, in infants it is more pronounced as a symptom of meningitis, tetanus or kernicterus. In emprosthotonus the head and feet are drawn forward with spine arches backward.

Fig: 4.5 Bending Posture in Opisthotonus

HANU GRAHA :

हनुमूल स्थितो बन्धात् संस्रयत्यनिलो हनू। विवृतास्यत्वमथवा कुर्यात् स्तब्धमवेदनम्।।

हनग्रुहं च संस्तभ्य हनुं (नू) संवृतवक्रताम्। (च.चि.28/49)

When root of jaw/mandible is affected by *vata* then it causes jaws to slip down from their joints resulting in opening of the mouth, stiffening of mandibles consequently closes mouth. The stiffness of mandible is present along with absence of pain.

In modern view, the lock jaw is associated symptom with the tetanus, is a serious bacterial disease that affects muscles and nerves. It is characterized by muscle stiffness that usually involves jaw, neck that progresses to involve other parts of body. Death can result from the severe breathing difficulties or heart abnormalities.

Temporo mandibular joint:

The temporo mandibular joint (TMJ) is a modified hinge type of synovial joint, permitting gliding (translation) and a small degree of rotation in addition to flexion (elevation) and extension (depression) movements typical for hinge joints.

The bony articular surfaces involved are the mandibular fossa and articular tubercle of the temporal bone superiorly, and the head of the mandible inferiorly. The bony articular surfaces are completely separated by fibrocatilage & articular disc of the TMJ.

Ligaments involved are:

- Fibrous capsule
- Lateral or temporo mandibular ligament
- Spheno mandibular ligament
- Stylo mandibular ligament

Movements at joint:

The movement at joint can be divided into those related to upper articular surface and articular disc i.e; meniscotemporal compartment & those between disc and head of mandible, i.e; menisco mandibular compartment.

In slight opening (depression) the head of mandible moves on the under surface of the disc like a hinge. In protraction, the movement is followed by gliding of disc and head of mandible. At the end, the head come close to lie under articular tubercle. The movements are reversed on closing the mouth or elevation of mandible.

Even as mentioned by Moore, the sideway blow to the chin when the mouth is open dislocates the TMJ on the side received the blow. Fractures are common of mandibles on blow or fall and associated with traumatic dislocations and rupture of the articular capsule and lateral ligaments leading to unstable condition of the joint.

The above cited diseases mostly bear a resemblance to tetanus. It results in severe, uncontrollable muscle spasms. Tetanus can be localized or generalized along with sign &symptoms. The affected cases represent similar symptoms like extensor rigidity, abnormal facial expression, dysphagia, and increased tongue tone with risus sardonicus.

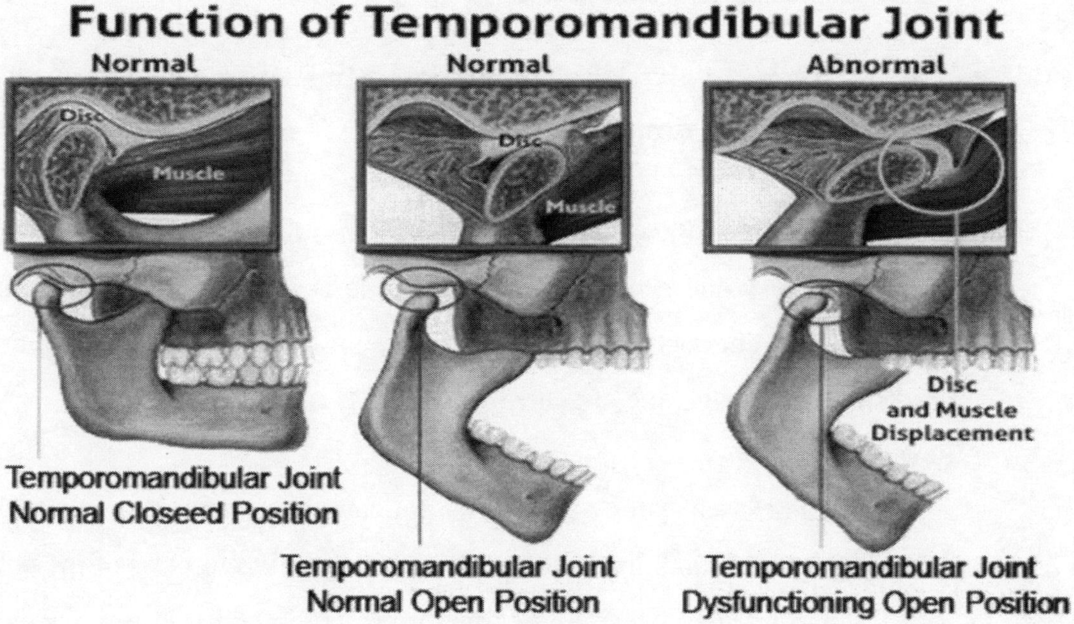

Fig: 4.6 The Temporomandibular Joint

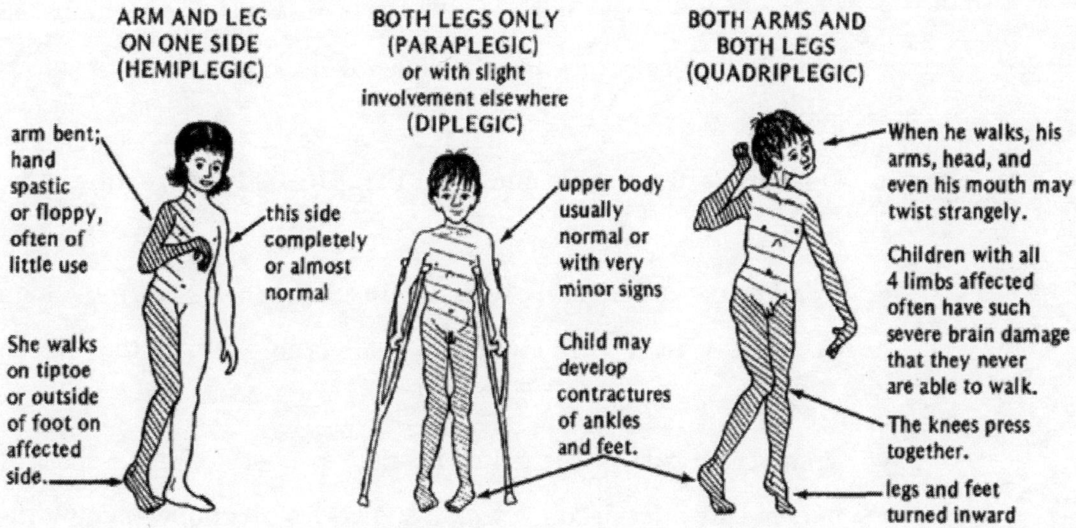

Fig: 4.7 Showing Types of Paralysis

EKA AND SARVANGA ROGA:

गृहीत्वाऽर्धं शरीरस्य सिराः स्नायूर्विशोष्य च।पादं सङ्कोचयत्येकं हस्तं वा तोदशूलकृत्।
एकाङ्गरोगं तं विद्यात् सर्वाङ्गं सर्वदेहजम्।। (च.चि.28/53-55)

When *vata* affects half of the body, it also affects blood vessels and ligaments, so paralysis of one-side occurs (right/left). There is loss of movement, speech and pain is present. When contraction is confined to one of the foot -hand with pain and distress. It results in *ekangaroga* and at generalized level it is *sarvanga roga.*

Paralysis:

The different types of paralysis are caused as a result of injury being located in different places around the spine and so affecting different parts of the body.

- Quadriplegia: affecting all four limbs, trunk and this is a result of spinal injury occurring above thoracic vertebrae.
- Paraplegia: caused by the injury located below the thoracic vertebrae, resulting in loss of movement in both legs. For Example: a person sitting in the chair due to spinal injury.
- Monoplegia: Spinal injury that affects just one of the limbs, usually a result of damage to localize areas of peripheral nervous system or corresponding parts of motor cortex.
- Diplegia: affects to symmetrical parts of body, normally both arms or sides of face.
- Hemiplegia: affects only one side resulting in loss of movement down one side. Commonly by a result of stroke affecting one of the hemisphere in brain – opposite side of brain.
- Transection of spinal cord results in loss of all sensation and voluntary movements inferior to the lesion and above mentioned symptoms may occur.

GRITHARSI :

स्फिक्पूर्वा कटिपृष्ठोरुजानुजङ्घापदं क्रमात्। गृध्रसी स्तम्भरुक्तोदैर्गृह्णाति स्पन्दते मुहुः।।
वाताद् वातकफात् तन्द्रागौरवारोचकान्विता। (च.चि.28/56-57)

The *vata vyadhi* which starts from hip gradually comes down to waist, back, thigh, knee, shank, foot etc. With the signs like stiffness, distress, piercing pain, frequent quickening. Along with *vata dosha* there is presence of *kapha* which results in drowsiness, heaviness and anorexia.

Normal Anatomy of Sciatic Nerve:

The sciatic nerve is the thickest nerve in body (2cm wide). The root value is L4, L5, S1, S2 and S3. It leaves the pelvis via the greater sciatic foramen below piriformis and descends between the greater trochanter and ischial tuberosity, along the back of the thigh. It divides into tibial and common peroneal (fibular) nerves. The division of the sciatic nerve into its major components (tibial and common peroneal) is variable.

The common site is at junction of the middle and lower thirds of the thigh, near apex of the popliteal fossa.

Sciatica:

Sciatica describes the condition in which patients have pain along the sensory distribution of the sciatic nerve. Thus, the pain is experienced in the posterior aspect of the thigh, the posterior and lateral sides of the leg, and the lateral part of the foot.

Sciatica can be caused by prolapse of an intervertebral disc with pressure on one or more roots of the lower lumbar and sacral spinal nerves, pressure on the sacral plexus or sciatic nerve by an intra pelvic tumor, or inflammation of the sciatic nerve or its terminal branches.

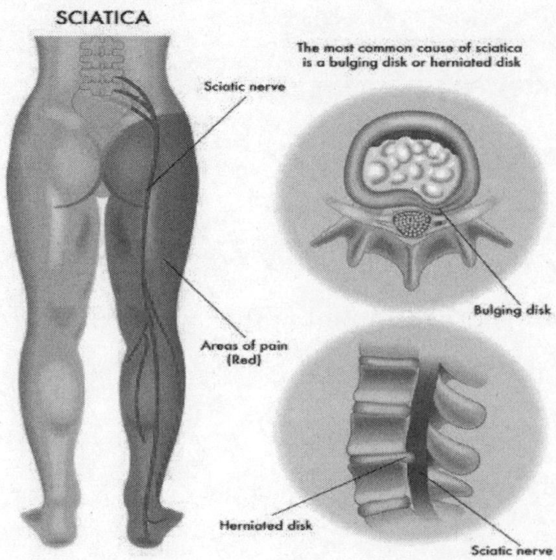

Fig: 4.8 Showing the Sciatica Affected Region

In such condition, the vertebral column shows a scoliosis, with its concavity on the side of the lesion. Pain is referred down the leg and foot in the distribution of the affected nerve. Since the sensory posterior roots most commonly pressed on are the fifth lumbar and the first sacral, pain is usually felt down the back and lateral side of the leg, radiating to the sole of the foot. This condition is often called **sciatica.**

Hence, it is a verified fact that *Vayu* is the only factor for information from one point to the other. Similarly, the signal (through nerves) controls our bodily functions and must be prevented from injuries.

KEYS POINTS:

- *Uttamangiya Sharir* is concerned with nervous system and importance of it being the residence of *Prana.*
- *Shira* (head) is crucial organ where all sense organs & their receptors reside. It is also among the "Tripod of Life".
- Each disease with possible association to modern relation has been done. Examples include *Ardita* (facial paralysis), *Akeshpa* & *Dandaka* (convulsive movements), *Hanu graha* (temporo-mandibular joint), *Gritharsi* (sciatica).
- Basically highlights the important role of *Vata* with relation to nervous system.

REVIEW ON UDARAGATA ROGA

(THE ALIMENTARY SYSTEM)

Introduction:

The abdomen is part of trunk between thorax and pelvis. It is a flexible, dynamic container, housing most of the organs of alimentary system and part of urogenital system. The area where almost all organs (especially related to digestion) reside is known as *Udara* (abdomen).

Etymology:

- The word "*Udara*" is derived from "ॠ" *Dhatu* prefixing with "उत्" and suffixing it with "अच्" *Pratya*.

उत् +ॠ+अच्। अन्तयलोपञ्च।

उदरं (क्ली) उत् ॠणातीति। उदिहणातेरजलौपुर्ब्बपदान्त्यलोपञ्च।

- In *Shabdha kalpadrooma*, the following etymology is defined,

नाभिस्तनयोर्मध्यभागः। पेट इति भाषा (श.क.द्रु. भाग)

- In *Amarkosha udara* word is illustrated as

पिचिण्डः कुक्षी जठरोदरं तुन्दम्। (अ.का.)

- Sir Monier Williams enumerated *Udara* as belly, abdomen, stomach, bowel, womb, a cavity, hollow, and interior or inside of anything.

उदर के पर्याय (Synonyms):

- उदर, महास्त्रोत,अग्निस्थान, कोष्ठ, अन्नवहस्त्रोत,पिचिण्डः, कुक्षी, कुक्षि, जठर, पेट, तुन्दम्

  कोष्ठ, महास्त्रात, शरीरमध्यं , महानिम्नं, आमपक्वाशय

- पञ्चदश कोष्ठाङ्गानि,कोष्ठः पुनरूच्यते महास्त्रोतः शरीरमध्यं महानिम्नं आमपक्वाशयश्चेति पर्या यशब्दैस्तन्त्रे स रोगमार्ग आभ्यन्तरः। (च.सू.11/48)

Acharya Charaka has mentioned above synonymous words to abdominal region in reference to pathways of diseases.

Kosthanga:

पञ्चदश कोष्ठाङ्गानि, तद्यथा -नाभिश्च, हृदयं च, क्लोम च, यकृच्च, प्लीहा च, वृक्कौ च,
बस्तिश्च, पुरीषाधारश्च, आमाशयश्च, पक्वाशयश्च, उत्तरगुदं च, अधरगुदं च,
क्षुद्रान्त्रं च स्थूलान्त्रं च, वपावहनं चेति।। (च. शा.7/10)

The number of visceral organs present in the middle part (*Kostha*) are said to be 15. These are *Nabhi* (navel), *Hridaya* (heart), *Kloma*, *Yakrit* (liver), *Pleeha* (spleen) , *Vrikka* (kidney), *Basti* (urinary bladder), *Purishadara* (caecum), *Aamashya* (stomach), *Pakvashya*(jejunum), Utaraguda (rectum), *Adharaguda* (anus), *Shudrantra* (small intestines), *Sthulaantra* (large intestine) and *Vapavahan* (omentum).

It is illustrated in the contemporary science that many of the diseases particularly the abdominal diseases arise from defect of *Agni* (*Jatharagni Bala*). There is increased vitiation of *Mala* and *Dosha*. The occurrence of *Udaragata Roga* is entirely based on the power of digestion. *Acharya Charaka* has enumerated eight types of *Udara Roga* in chapter 13th of *Chikitsa Sthana.*

कुक्षेराध्मानमाटोपः शोफः पादकरस्य च।

मन्दोऽग्निः श्लक्ष्णगण्डत्वं कार्श्यं चोदरलक्षणम्।। (च.चि.13/21)

The common symptoms present in the *Udara Roga* are *Aadhmana* (tympanitis), *Aatopa* (gurgling sound), *Shotha* (edema of limbs), *Agni Mandha* (poor digestion), *Slakshna Galganda* (smooth cheek), and *Karshya* (emanciation).

Following diseases are discussed in this section under *Udara Roga* with the possible modern correlation.

DISEASES RELATED TO UDARA

PLEEHODARA:

Among the eight *Udara Rogas*, *Plehodara* (splenic disorders) is described by *Acharya Charaka* as follows.

वामपार्श्वाश्रितः प्लीहा च्युतः स्थानात् प्रवर्धते। शोणितं वा रसादिम्भ्यो विवृद्धं तं विवर्धयेत्।।
तस्य प्लीहा कठिनोऽष्ठीलेवादौ वर्धमानः कच्छपसंस्थान उपलभ्यते; .... प्लीहजठर
एवावरोध इति; एतत् प्लीहोदरमिति विद्यात्।।तस्य रूपाणि तदधो नाभेः प्रायोऽभिवर्धमानमुदकोदरं भवि
त, यथाबलं च दोषाणां ....उपवेशते, हिक्काश्वास कास-तृष्णाप्रमेहारोचकाविपाक
दौर्बल्यपरीतश्य भवति, एतच्छिद्रोदरमिति विद्यात्।। (च.चि.13/36-44)

The spleen is said to be on the left side and due to over weight lifting, strenuous exercises etc spleen gets displaced from the normal situation and is enlarged due to increased blood flow. Due to enlargement spleen is felt to be hard and gradually appears like as a tortoise. If left untreated, it overlaps abdominal region and thus affects the digestion process.

The signs and symptoms of *Pleehodara* indicates in debility, anorexia, indigestion, thirst, hardness of stool, body-ache, vomiting, dysponea, fever, emancipation, pain in small joints, appearance of streaks over abdomen. Similarly there is *Yakrit* (liver) on the right side having similar etiology, symptoms and treatments.

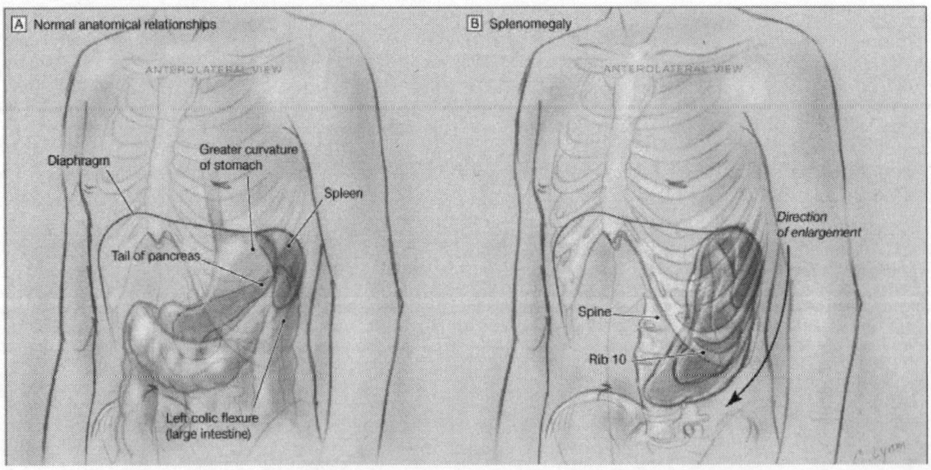

Figure: 5.1 Showing Spleenomegaly

Splenic Diseases:

Spleen is the largest ductless gland of haemo-lymph system. It plays essential role in the immune responses of the body.

Spleen is situated in left hypochondrium, epigastrium region. There are 2 angles; anterior basal and posterior basal angle. In case of spleen enlargement anterior basal angle (angle between superior border & lateral end) becomes palpable under left costal margin. It is known as **"clinical angle of spleen."**

The condition of splenomegaly occurs in typhoid, hemolytic anemia, malaria, portal hypertension, granulocytic leukemia. Rupture of spleen may arise due to severe blow or penetrating wound, increased intra abdominal pressure.

BADHAGUDUDARA:

पक्ष्मबालैः सहान्नेन भुक्तैर्बद्धायने गुदे। उदावर्तैस्तथाऽर्शोभिरन्त्रसम्मूर्च्छनेन वा।।
अपानो मार्गसंरोधाद्धत्वाग्निं कुपितोऽनिलः। वर्चः पित्तकफान् रुद्ध्वा जनयत्युदरं ततः।।

(च.चि.13/39)

This condition may arise due to intake of eyelashes (probably hair) in food, there is obstruction in anal passage, reverse peristalsis starts, piles, intussusceptions (tangled intestines), and retention of faeces. There are mostly similar signs of abdominal disorders that are anorexia, vomiting, debility, indigestion, retention of stool-urine, pain in head, heart and navel region.

CHIDRODARA:

शर्करातृणकाष्ठास्थिकण्टकैरन्नसंयुतैः। भिद्येतान्त्रं यदा भुक्तैर्जृम्भयाऽत्यशनेन वा।।
पाकं गच्छेद्रसस्तेभ्यश्छिद्रेभ्यः प्रस्रवद् बहिः। पूरयन् गुदमन्त्रं च जनयत्युदरं ततः।।

(च.चि.13/42-43)

Due to intake of gravels, wooden or bony pieces with food, they irritate the visceral membranes and due to perforation the juices of abdomen (chyle) spreads out into intestinal spaces.

The umbilicus gets protruded, the patient passes stool with blood, hiccups, dysponea, cough, polyuria, anorexia and debility. The symptoms are similar to perforative abdomen or peritonitis.

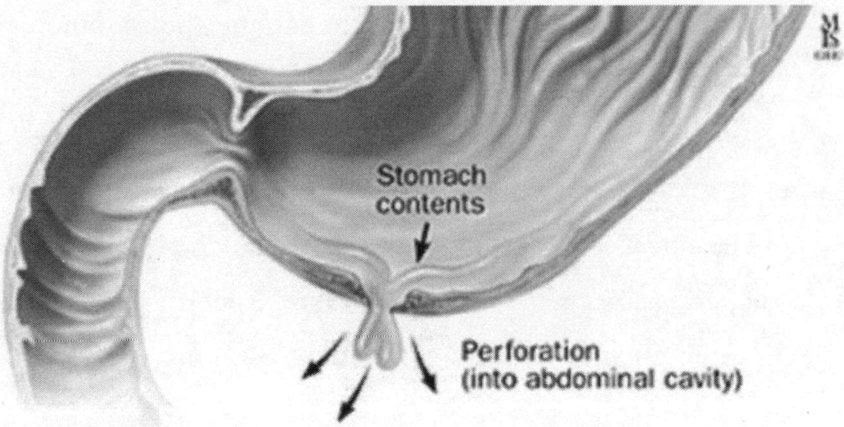

Fig: 5.1 Showing Gastric Content Perforation

Surgical aspect:

वामं कुक्षिं मापयित्वा नाभ्यधश्चतुरङ्गुलम् ।मात्रायुक्तेन शस्त्रेण पाटयेनमतिमान भिषक्।।
विपाटयन्त्रं ततः पश्चाद्वीक्ष्य बद्धक्षतान्त्रयोः। सर्पिषाऽभ्यज्य केशादीनवमृज्य विमोक्षयेत्।
मूर्च्छनाद्यच्च संमूढमन्त्रं तच्च विमोक्षयेत् ।। छिद्राण्यन्त्रस्य तु स्थूलैर्दंशयित्वा पिपीलिकैः।
बहुशः संगृहीतानि ज्ञात्वा छित्वा पिपीलिकान्।।प्रतियोगैः प्रवैश्यान्त्रं प्रेयैःसीव्येद् व्रणं ततः।
(च.चि.13/184-187)

Acharya Charaka mentioned the operative procedure for the treatment of *Badhagududara* (obstructive) and *Chidrodara* (perforative) abdominal disorders. After measuring four fingers below the umbilicus on the left side the wise physician should incise with measured instrument. After opening the abdomen, the intestines should be examined for obstruction or perforation. By lubricating the loops he should remove the interlocking. If holes of perforation persists then they should be got bitten by the large ants and only their heads must be left when they stick tightly. After this restore intestines in place and suturing by needles must be done.

Above mentioned condition of *Badhagududara* (obstructive) and *Chidrodara* (perforative) have similar medical conditions. Mostly these affect the bowels (intestines) and produce medical emergency. The most common site for a variety of benign and malignant tumours is originating from epithelial lining. Benign tumour presents clinically a polyp. A polyp is defined as any growth or mass protruding from the mucous membrane.

If we take condition of intestinal obstruction or peritonitis the widespread causes are due to intussusceptions, volvolus, tumours, or foreign material. Intussusception is telescoping of a segment of intestine below due to peristalsis. This condition is common in infants or young children. In ileoceacal region when the portion of ileum invaginates into ascending colon without affecting ileoceacal valve.

The complication can be added due to volvolus, the twisting of intestinal loop upon itself. It leads to obstruction and blood supply is cut off for the affected part. The poor food habits, little roughage in diet, lack of exercise result in low bowel movement & creates problem in gut.

Peritonitis is the inflammation of the peritoneum due to micro organisms or some chemicals. Even the internal secretion of enzymes, juices can cause inflammation.

<u>JALODHARA</u>:

तस्य रूपाणि - अनन्नकाङ्क्षापिपासागुदस्रावशूलश्वासकासदौर्बल्यानि, अपि चोदरं नानावर्ण राजि सिरा सन्ततमुदकपूर्णदृतिक्षोभसंस्पर्शं भवति, ...स्वस्थानादपवृत्ताः परिपाकाद् द्रवीभूताः सन्धीन् स्रोतांसि चोपक्लेदयन्ति, स्वदेश्च बाह्येषु स्रोतः सु प्रतिहतगति स्तिर्यगवतिष्ठमानस्तदेवोदकमाप्यायययति .... ततोऽनन्तरमुदकप्रादुर्भावः। तस्य रूपाणि - कुक्षेरतिमात्रवृद्धिः, सिराऽन्तर्धानगमनम्, उदकपूर्णदृतिसङ्क्षोभसंस्पर्शत्वं च।। (च.चि.13/47-48)

When there is accumulation of fluid in abdomen due to the vitiation of *doshas* (*Vata*, *Kapha*) and affects *Kloma* and by the fluid there is obstruction in the channels. So the fluid mostly gets accumulated into the abdomen.

Symptoms which are present in the patient are discharge from anal region, pain, dysponea, debility and presence of streaks over the abdomen. On palpation there are fluctuations like in water filled balloon.

If left untreated it may include *Sandhi* (joint), and *Srotas* (channels). There is dull appearance on percussion, soft when palpated and streak less on inspection. The severity of disease keeps on increasing with time if not properly treated.

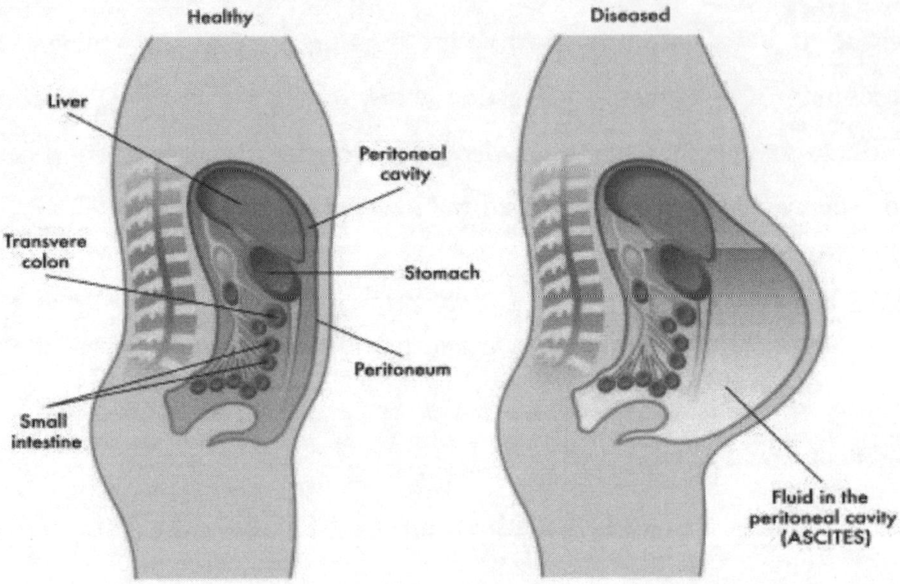

Fig: 5.2 Showing the Ascitis Condition

Ascitis:

The condition of peritonitis occurs when an ulcer perforates the wall of stomach or duodenum, spilling acid content into the peritoneal cavity. Excess fluid in the peritoneal cavity is called as ascitic fluid. The clinical condition results in ascites. The collection of fluid in the cavity interferes with the movement of viscera. Portal hypertension affects the peritoneal cavity with liters of fluid accumulated in the cavity known as ascitis.

In severe portal obstruction, the veins of the anterior abdominal wall that anastomosis with the para umbilical veins may become varicose and look somewhat like snakes radiating under skin around umbilicus and is called as "caput medusae".

BRADHNA :

ब्रन्धोऽनिलाद्यैर्वृषणे स्वलिङ्गैरन्त्रं निरेति प्रविशेन्मुहुश्च।
मूत्रण पूर्णं मृदु मेदसा चेत् स्निग्धं च विद्यात् कठिनं च शोथम्।।
विरेचनाभ्यङ्गनिरूहलेपाः पक्वेषु चैव व्रणवच्चिकित्सा।
स्यान्मूत्रमेदः कफजं विपाट्य विशोध्य सीव्येद् व्रणवच्च पक्वम्।।

(च.चि.12/94-95)

Acharya Charaka has mentioned the concept of *Bradhna* (inguinal hernia) where intestines comes out into scrotal or inguinal region and for the *Mutra Roga* in relation to enlargement of the scrotum and fluid accumulation (hydrocele). This happens due to the vitiation of respective *Doshas*.

The Normal Anatomy of Inguinal Canal:

The inguinal canal is a natural hiatus in the tissues of the anterior abdominal wall, and is formed from the various layers of the wall in the region of the groin.

The canal is an oblique tunnel, with deep and superficial openings (or rings). It varies in size and form with age and more developed in males.

Boundaries:

- Anterior wall:

  External oblique aponeurosis, reinforced laterally by the origin of the internal oblique from the inguinal ligament. This wall is therefore strongest where it lies opposite the weakest part of the posterior wall, namely, the deep inguinal ring.

- Posterior wall:

  Conjoint tendon medially, fascia transversalis laterally. This wall is, therefore strongest where it lies opposite the weakest part of the anterior wall, namely, the superficial inguinal ring.

- Roof or superior wall: Arching lowest fibers of the internal oblique and transversus abdominis muscles.

- Floor or inferior wall: Upturned lower edge of the inguinal ligament and, at its medial end, the lacunar ligament.

1. <u>The superficial (external) inguinal ring:</u>

It is exit by which the spermatic cord in males or the round ligament in females emerges from the inguinal canal. The ring is a split that occurs in the diagonal, otherwise parallel fibers of the external oblique aponeurosis just supero lateral to the pubic tubercle. The superficial inguinal ring is only a distinct aperture when the continuity of this fascia with the aponeurosis is interrupted. The ring is smaller in females.

2. <u>The deep (internal) inguinal ring:</u>

It is the entrance of the inguinal canal. It is located superior to the middle of the inguinal ligament and lateral to the inferior epigastric artery. It is the beginning of envagination in the transversalis fascia which forms an opening. Through this opening the vas deferens and testicular vessels (in males) and round ligament of uterus (in females) pass to enter the inguinal canal.

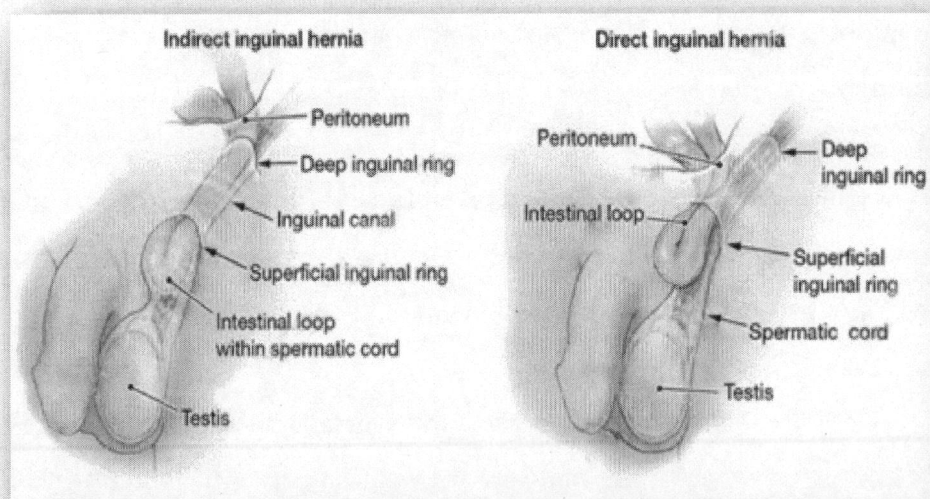

Fig: 5.3 Showing Types of Hernia

Applied anatomy:

The processus vaginalis (diverticulum of peritoneal cavity) forms a communicating channel between the peritoneal cavity within the abdomen & tunica vaginalis within the scrotum. If the opening does not close (during 1st year of life) then the intestinal loops may descend to the scrotum.

Inguinal hernia involves the protrusion of a viscous through the tissues of the inguinal region of the abdominal wall. The majority of herniation occurs in this region (75%). The two types of inguinal hernias are ***direct*** and ***indirect hernia.***

Following table enlists the features of both types.

Characteristics	Direct(acquired)	Indirect (congenital)
Predisposing factors	Weakness of anterior abdominal wall in inguinal triangle.	Patency of processus vaginalis (specially in young ones)
Frequency	Less common	More common
Exit from abdominal cavity.	Peritoneum along with transversalis fascia	Peritoneum of persistent processus vaginalis along with coverings of cord or ligament.
Course	Passes through or around inguinal canal, external & parallel to vestige of processus vaginalis.	Traverses inguinal canal within the processus vaginalis.
Exit from anterior abdominal wall	Via superficial ring, lateral to cord, rarely enters scrotum	Via superficial ring inside cord, commonly passing into scrotum/labium majus.

Table: 5.1Types of Inguinal Hernia

MUTRA VRIDHI :

Acharya Charaka says that the scrotal enlargement due to *Mutra* is soft and due to fat it may be hard on touching.

A condition, where there is collection fluid in some parts of processus vaginalis is called hydrocele. It is of four types:

HYDROCELE

VAGINAL: collection of fluid in tunica vaginalis testis. This may be primary or secondary to some disease of testis or epidydmis.

CONGENITAL: a congenital hernia sac between processus vaginalis and peritoneal cavity, which permits fluid in abdominal cavity.

INFANTILE: the processus vaginalis is occluded at internal abdominal ring only.

HYDROCELE OF THE CORD: the funicular process fails to shrink into a fibrous cord, so that a tubular cavity results. It becomes distended with fluid.

Flowchart: 5.1 Showing Types of Hydrocele

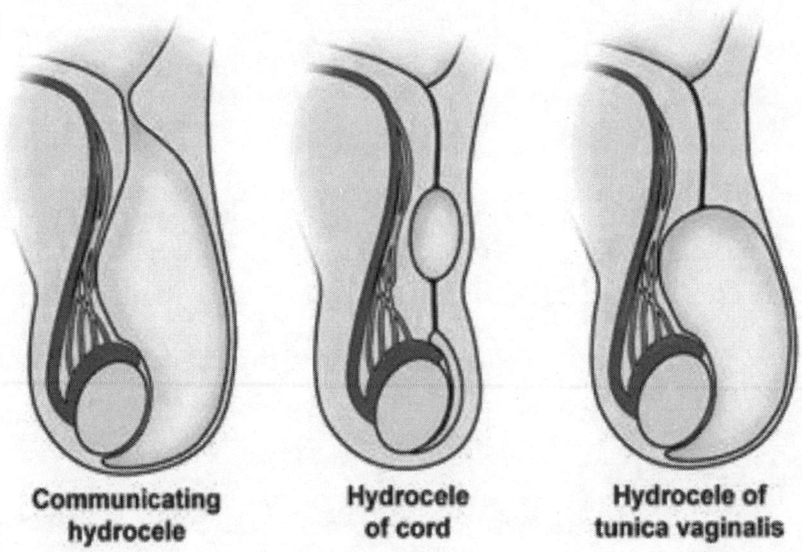

Fig: 5.4 Showing Different Conditions of Hydrocele

The above mentioned condition may be associated with an indirect inguinal hernia. A hydrocele of the testis is confined to scrotum and distends the tunica vaginalis and the other related to the spermatic cord and distends persistent part of stalk of processus vaginalis.

KEYS POINTS:

- This section deals with reflections of the anatomical as well as surgical view of *Acharya Charaka.*
- With no reference to dissection mentioned in text he has clearly given concept of surgical procedure using *Pipplika* (large ants).
- Most of diseases here are those which have surgical side (*pleehodara, jalodhara, chidrodara* etc).

REVIEW ON GUDAGATA ROGA

(ANO RECTAL REGION)

Introduction:

In the present scenario, the sedentary life style, irregular and inappropriate diet, prolonged sitting and stressful life are important causes in pathogenesis of ano-rectal diseases. Along with this the main factor is considered to be improper functioning of *Jathragni* (power of digestion).

Guda has been enumerated among fifteen *Kosthanga* of the body by *Acharya Charaka* and divide into parts (*Uttara Guda & Adhara Guda*). *Chakrapani* explains that former is the seat of faecal material collection whereas later helps the evacuator. It has also been included in *Dasha Pranayatana.*

दश प्राणायतनानि तद्यथा- मूर्धा, कण्ठः, हृदयं, नाभिः, गुदं, बस्तिः, ओजः, शुक्रं,
शोणितं, मांसमिति। (च.शा.7/9)

Etymology:

The word *"Guda"* is derived from following *Dhatu*

"ङ खेलने (कविकल्पद्रुमः)

ङ गोदते (दुर्गादासः)

- In *Shabada kalpadrooma*, the word "*Guda*" is enumerated as
  गोदते खेलति चलतीत्यर्थः अपानसज्ञंकवायुः अनेन। गुद् + इ गुपधेति।। (श.क.द्रु. भाग)
- In *Shabadstoma*, the word "*Guda*" is enumerated as
  मलत्यागद्वारे अपानवायुनिस्सारणद्वारे।
- In *Vachaspatyama*, "*Guda*" refers as
  गुदः खेले भ्वारू आत्मरूअकरू सेद्। गोदते अगोदिष्ट। जुगुदे। गुदम्। (वा.)
- In *Parishadya Shabdartha Shariram* describes the etymology as,

गुयतेऽनेनेति गुदमिति पुरीषोत्सर्गार्थकगुधातोर्निष्पन्नेनैव गुद क्रीडायाम् त गु मलोत्सर्गे।

(पारिषद्यं शब्दाथ शारीरम्)

गुद के पर्याय (Synonyms):

Following are the synonyms which are used to indicate the *Guda* (anal canal).

पायु, अपान, मलत्यागद्वार, मलायतन, गुह्यम्

NORMAL ANATOMY OF THE ANAL CANAL:

The anal canal is lower terminal part of the alimentary canal. It is situated in anal triangle of perineum between right-left ischio-rectal fossae and below pelvic diaphragm. The approx. length of canal is 4cm.

Peculiarities of the anal canal:

- It is surrounded by the inner involuntary and outer voluntary sphincters.
- There are surgical spaces related to anal canal like ischio rectal space, perianal space and sub mucous space.

Internal structure of the anal region is divisible into **3** parts.

- ❖ The upper part is about 15mm long, 6-10 anal columns are present, valves of morgagni, anal papillae, anal sinuses.
- ❖ The intermediate part is also 15mm long and situated between pectinate and Hilton's line.
- ❖ The lower part is near about 8mm in length and situated below Hilton's line. The sphincters present in the anal canal are sphincter ani internus and sphincter ani externus.

An ano rectal ring is also present at ano rectal junction. The arterial supply is done by superior rectal artery (above pectinate line) and inferior rectal artery (below pectinate line).

The venous drainage is important to discuss because it results into pathological condition. The internal rectal venous plexus are the site for formation of primary internal piles. The external venous plexus may get rupture due to straining during defecation and results in external piles.

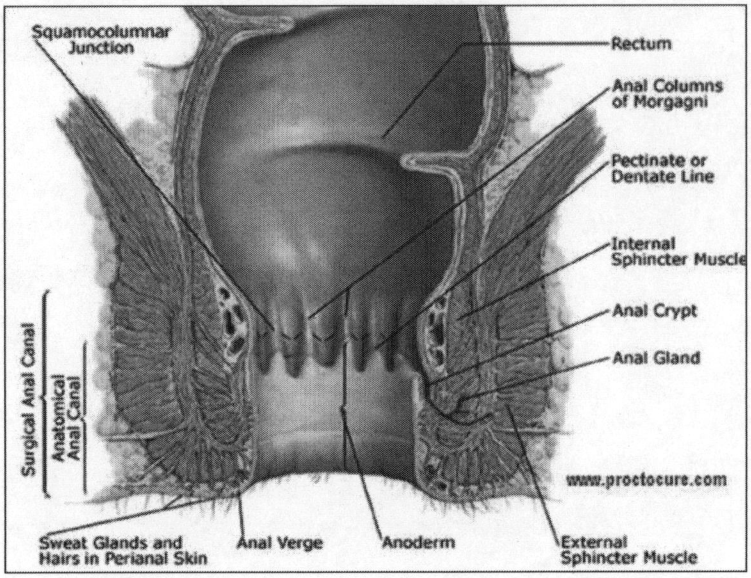

Fig: 6.1 Showing Normal Anatomy of Anal Canal

The diseases of this region are mainly based on the diet ingredients, lifestyles and psychological disturbances etc. that leads to vitiation of *Dosha.* Along with this the resultant is disturbed digestion and it results into constipation and related diseases.

DISEASES RELATED TO GUDA REGION

BHAGANDARA :

क्रिम्यस्थिसूक्ष्मक्षणनव्यवायप्रवाहणान्युत्कटकाश्वपृष्ठैः।
गुदस्य पार्श्वे पिडका भृशार्तिः पक्वप्रभिन्नास्तु भगन्दरः स्यात्।।
(च.चि.12/96)

A little description is given about *Bhagandara* in the chapter of *Shotha Chikitsa.* Due to the unhygienic condition of anal region, sexual intercourse, straining during defecation and many other causes may lead to occurrence of *Pidika* (boils) in the anal region. These are very painful suppurate and breaks out easily. There is pus discharge and is related to fistula-in-ano.

Fistula in ano:

Bailey & Love has stated that fistula-in-ano is a tract lined by granulation tissue which opens deeply in the anal canal or rectum and superficially on the skin around the anus.

A fistula is a tract communicating with two surfaces, either mucosa to mucosa; mucosa to skin. The majority of anal fistulae start as an anal inter sphincter abscess secondary to infection of inter muscular anal glands.

The modern concept of fistula-in-ano is based on its anatomical considerations. External sphincter and levator ani muscle are the fixed landmarks to describe the relation and course taken by the fistulous track.

It can be classified into four types: "Parks Classification System".

1. Inters phincteric
2. Trans-sphincteric
3. Supra-sphincteric
4. Extra sphincteric

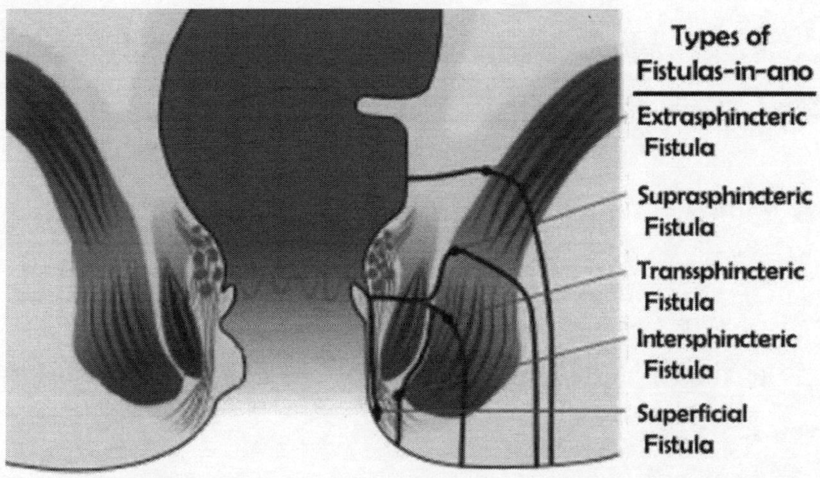

Fig: 6.2 Showing Types of Fistula In Ano

In some cases, while removing the fistulous tracks damage to the ano rectal ring occurs and results in rectal incontinence.

ARSHA :

सर्वेषां चार्शसां क्षेत्रं - गुदस्यार्धपञ्चमाङ्गलावकाशे त्रिभागान्तरास्तिस्रो गुदवलयः क्षेत्रमिति; केचित्तु भूयांसमेव देशमुपदिशत्यर्शसां शिश्नमपत्यपथं गलतालुमुखनासिकाकर्णाक्षिवर्त्मानि त्वक् चेति। तदस्त्यधिमांसदेशतया, गुदवलिजानां त्वर्शांसीति संज्ञा तन्त्रेऽस्मिन्।
सर्वेषां चार्श-सामधिष्ठानं -मेदो मांसं त्वक् च।।अर्शांसि खलु जायन्ते नासन्निपतितैस्त्रिभिः। दोषैदोर्षैविशेषात्तु विशेषः कल्प्यतेऽर्शसाम्।। पञ्चात्मा मारूतः पित्तं कफो गुदवलित्रयम्। सर्व एव प्रकुप्यन्ति गुदजानां समुद्भवे।। (च.चि.14/6,23-24)

The location to all types of *Arsha* (piles) is the three ano-rectal folds. Each fold is situated in space of 5 and 1/2 fingers each at distance of 1/3 of above. They are considered to be fleshy outgrowth but basically the piles have- *Mamas* (flesh), *Medha* (fat) and *Twacha* (skin) involved.

According to *Acharya Charaka*, the vitiated *Dosha* follow *Bahya* and *Abhyantra Roga Marga* to produce *Arsha*. And he further describes that all types of *Vata, Pitta* and *Kapha* were affecting the *Twacha, Mansa* and *Medha* in *Gudavali* producing *Arsha Roga*.

Acharya Charaka has mentioned two types of *Arsha* as *Sahaja* (hereditary) and *Jatasyottarakalaja* (acquired) respectively.

Hemorrhoids (Piles):

The term hemorrhoids is derived from the Greek adjective 'haemorrhoids' meaning bleeding (haima= blood; rhoos= flowing). They are dilated veins within the anal canal in the subepithelial region formed by radicles of the superior, middle and inferior rectal veins.

Sr. No.	Types Of Haemorrhoids	
1.	Congenital type	Acquired type
2.	External	Internal

Table:6.1 Illustrating Types of Haemorrhoids

External hemorrhoids are thromboses (blood clots) in the vein of the external rectal plexuses and are covered by skin.

Internal hemorrhoids are prolapse of rectal mucosa (anal cushions) containing the normally dilated veins of the internal rectal venous plexus. They have bright red blood due to arteriovenous anastomoses.

In case of portal obstruction, the radicles of superior rectal vein passing through anal column in left lateral (3'o clock), right posterior (7'o clock) and right anterior (11'o clock) are distended earlier than other veins. These are sites for primary internal piles.

KEYS POINTS:

- The *Guda* (Anal region) is susceptible to various diseases due to intervention with external environment.
- The anatomical aspects like occurrence of *Bhagandara* and *Arsha* is due to infections in the region.
- The venous supply results in piles and mucous membrane is affected in fistula which is vulnerable to infections.

REVIEW ON BASTIGATA ROGA

(THE EXCRETORY SYSTEM)

Introduction:

The excretory system is defined as a group of organs which are responsible for excreting out the waste from the body. The system comprises of kidneys, bladder, ureters and urethra.

In *Ayurvedic* framework, V*rikka* and *Vpavahan* are the site organs in relation to *Medhovaha Srotas*. These are affected due to any disturbance of *Tridosha* and pathology occurs.

Etymology:

- In Shabada kalpa drooma, term "Basti" is derived from,

  वसति मूत्रादिकमत्र वस वसेति

- In shabadstoma, "Basti" is explained as,

  वस्ते आवृणोतिमूत्रं वसन्तिच। नाभेरधोभागे मूत्राधारे स्थाने।

  - Sir Monier Williams elucidated it as bladder, lower belly, abdomen & pelvis.

- According to *Kaviraja Gangadhara, "*V*rikka"* is defined as,

  वृक्कौ वृक्कद्वयम् वक्षोऽधस्तात्। (कविराज गंगाधर, च.शा.7/7)

- In *Amarkosha*, the following term is used for *"Basti"* and *"Vrikka"*

  नाभेरधोभागः ,वृक्काग्रमांसम् ।

मूत्राशय के पर्याय (Synonyms):

मूत्राशय, उदर,निवास, वृक्क, बस्ति

KOSTHANGA:

The organs mentioned in *Kostha* also comprise of *Vrikka* (kidney) and *Basti* (urinary bladder).

In *Vimana Sthana* chapter 5th, description of *Vrikka* and *Basti* are considered as *Moola Sthana* of *Medho Vaha* and *Mutra Vaha Srotas.* The pathogenesis of any disorder of these two channels affects the *Moola* organ.

Normal Anatomy Related To Excretory System:

The excretory system comprises of paired kidneys, 2 ureters, urinary bladder and urethra. The major function is to excrete the urine and remove toxins from body.

External features of kidneys:

Kidneys are the paired, retroperitoneal organ situated on the posterior abdominal wall on each side of vertebral column. The organ is bean-shaped & measuring about 11cm in length, 6cm in breadth and 3cm in thickness. It weighs near about 130-150gms.

Internal Structure of kidney:

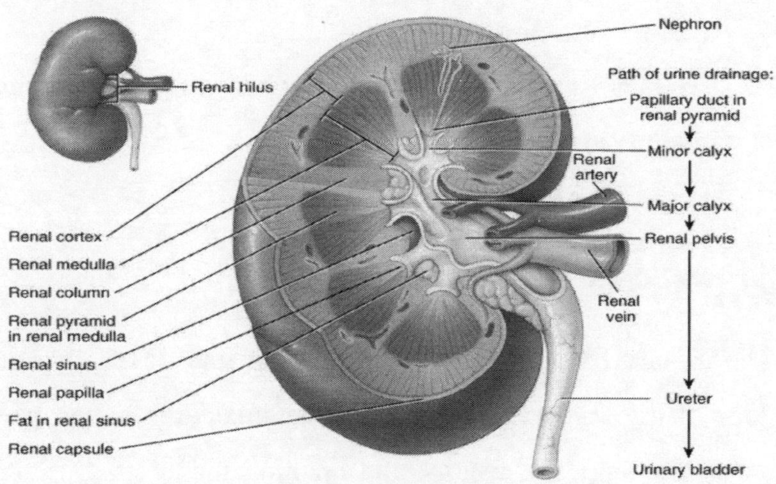

Figure: 7.1 Showing Internal Anatomy Of Kidney

By a coronal section of kidney, it reveals 2 distinct regions, superficial-light coloured renal cortex and deep- darker coloured renal medulla. Medulla consists of several cone-shaped renal pyramids and renal papilla [towards hilum].

Together, the renal cortex and pyramids of renal medulla constitute the parenchyma (functional portion) of kidney. Within this are the functional units of kidneys called as nephrons. Urine formed by nephrons drains into large papillary ducts which further drains the urine into cup-shaped structure known as calyces (minor & major). Major calyx drains into single large cavity known as renal pelvis & out through ureters to the urinary bladder.

Ureters:

These are paired narrow, thick walled muscular cylindrical tubes which convey urine to bladder from kidneys. These are about 25cm in length and normal diameter is 3mm. The ureters have a capacity of 5-7ml of urine (pelvis of ureter). Normally, there are few constrictions related to ureters which play major role in obstruction due to stone. These are:

- ✓ At pelvi-ureteric junction
- ✓ At brim of lesser pelvis
- ✓ Ureters crossing ductus deferens or broad ligament of uterus
- ✓ Obliquity at the bladder wall
- ✓ At opening in lateral angle of trigone

Urinary bladder:

The urinary bladder is hollow, muscular and distensible organ situated in pelvis. In the floor of urinary bladder is small triangular area called trigone. The ureters open at postero-lateral angles of trigone and opening for internal urethral orifice is located here. The capacity of an adult varies from 120-320ml.Normally, micturition occurs at 280ml and painful sensation arises at level above 500ml.Involuntary micturition occurs above 800ml.

Impact of nerve supply:

Urinary bladder is supplied by vesical plexus derived from inferior hypogastric plexus. Sensory sensations are carried by both sympathetic & parasympathetic nerves. In the spinal cord, pain arising in bladder passes through the lateral spinothalaminc tract, awareness is mediated by posterior columns. Bilateral antero-lateral cordotomy, therefore selectively abolishes pain without affecting the awareness of bladder distension & desire to micturate.

DISEASES RELATED TO MUTRAVAHA SANSTHANA

ASHMARI :

विशोषयेद्बस्तिगतं सशुक्रं मूत्रं सपित्तं पवनं कफं वा।

यदा तदाऽश्मर्युपजायते तु क्रमेण पित्तेष्विव रोचना गोः।। (च.चि.26/31)

In the chapter entitled *Trimarmiya-Chikitsye,* Acharya Charaka has mentioned the pathogenesis of calculus due to drying up of semen (*Shukra*), urine (*Mutra*) or *Pitta, Kapha.* It is similar in appearance to gall stone in cow.

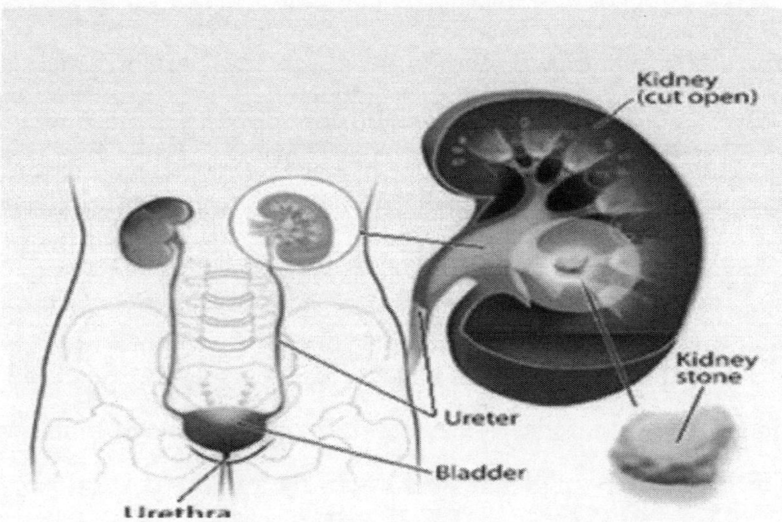

Fig: 7.2 Showing Calculus in Kidney

कदम्बपुष्पाकृतिरश्मतुल्या श्लक्ष्णा त्रिपुट्यप्यथवाऽपि मृद्वी।
मूत्रस्य चेन्मार्गमुपैति रुद्ध्वा मूत्रं रुजं तस्य करोति बस्तौ।।
ससेवनीमेहनबस्तिशूलं विशीर्णधारं च करोति मूत्रम्।
मृद्नाति मेढ्रं स तु वेदनार्तो मुहुः शकृन्मुञ्चति मेहते च।।
क्षोभात् क्षते मूत्रयतीह सासृक् तस्याः सुखं मेहति च व्यपायात्।
एषाऽश्मरी मारूतभिन्नमूर्तिः स्याच्छर्करा मूत्रपथात् क्षरन्ती।। (च.चि.26/32-34)

In the reference of *Ashmari* the description of pathogenesis along with types of calculus is mentioned. When calculus is like *Kadamba* flower, hard, smooth, prismatic or soft comes in passage of urine, and it obstructs the flow of urine and causes pain in bladder. There is pain in penis, bladder and related parts. The pain is sometimes of severe degree and patient can't control it. The calculus creates problem in passage of urine as it can produce condition of haematuria.

शुक्रं मलाश्चैव पृथक् पृथग्वा मूत्राश्यस्थाः प्रतिवारयन्ति । तद् व्याहतं मेहनबस्तिशूलं मूत्रं सशुक्रं कुरूते विबद्धम् ।। स्तब्धश्च शूनो भृशवेदनश्च तुद्येत बस्तिर्वृषणौ तु तस्य।

(च. चि.26/35)

The condition of *Mutrakrchha (Shukraja)* the discharge of semen by *Doshas* separately situated in the urinary bladder produce pain in phallus and pelvis, difficultly in passing of urine mixed with semen and the patient's pelvis as well as testicles get stiffened, swollen and intensely painful.

क्षताभिघातात् क्षतजं क्षयाद्वा प्रकोपितं बस्तिगतं विबद्धम्।
तीव्रार्ति मूत्रेण सहाल्पमल्पमायाति तस्मिन्नतिसञ्चिते च।।
आध्माततां विन्दति गौरवं च विनिःसृतेऽस्मिन्।। (च. चि.26/36-37)

Due to any injury in the tract (loss of semen also) blood discharged within urinary bladder is bound up and cause agonizing pain. After it binds with urine to form calculus and results in heaviness and swelling of the region. It is said as *Raktaj Mutrakrchha.*

BASTI ROGA:

In the perspective of *Basti Marma* in chapter 9th of *Siddhi Sthana* there is description of 13 types of urinary tract diseases.

मूत्रौकसादो जठरं कृच्छमुत्सङ्गसंक्षयौ। मूत्रातीतोऽनिलाष्ठीला वातबस्त्युष्णमारूतौ।।
वातकुण्डलिका ग्रन्थिर्विड्घतो बस्तिकुण्डलम्। त्रयोदशैते मूत्रस्य दोषास्ताँल्लिङ्गतः श्रृणु।।

(च.सि.9/25-26)

Mutraukasada, Mutrajathara, Mutrakrchha, Mutrotsanga, Mutrasamksaya, Mutratita, Vatastihla, Vatabasti, Usnavata, Vatakundalika, Granthi, Vidghata and *Bastikundala*- these are the 13 disorders of urine.

Sr.No.	Types Of Mutra Roga	Possible Modern Correlation
1.	मूत्रौकसाद (*Mutraukasada)*	Scanty urination, oliguria
2.	मूत्रजठर (*Mutrajathara)*	Distended bladder
3.	मूत्रकृच्छ (*Mutrakrchha*)	Dsyuria, painful micturition
4.	मूत्रौत्सङ्ग (*Mutrotsanga*)	Stricture of urethra
5.	मूत्रसंक्षय (*Mutrasamksaya*)	Anuria, suppression of urine
6.	मूत्रातीता (*Mutratita*)	Incontinence of urine
7.	अनिलाष्ठीला (*Vatastihla*)	Enlarged prostate
8.	वातबस्ति (*Vatabasti*)	Retention of urine
9.	उष्णमारूतौ (*Usnavata*)	Urinary infection
10.	वातकुण्डलिका (*Vatakundalika)*	Spasmodic stricture
11.	मूत्रग्रन्थि (*Granthi*)	Tumor, due to stone
12.	विड्घात (*Vidghata*)	Recto vesical fistula
13.	बस्तिकुण्डल (*Bastikundala*)	Atonic condition of bladder

Table: 7.1 Illustrating Types of *Mutra Rogas*

अनिलाष्ठीला (*Vatastihla*):

आध्मापयन् बस्तिगुदं रूद्ध्वा वायुश्चलोन्नताम्।
कुर्यात्तोव्रार्तिमष्ठीलां मूत्रविण्मार्गरोधिनीम्।। (च.सि. 9/36)

In condition of *Vatastihla,* the *Vata Dosha* creates obstruction in urinary bladder and anal region. There is production of stony mass (moveable), protruded, extremely painful and causing obstruction in passage of urine and stool.

Clinical Features Of Enlarged Prostate :

Benign Prostrate Hyperplasia (BPH) is a noncancerous enlargement of prostrate that blocks flows of urine through urethra.

- Narrowing of urethra, leads to contraction of bladder forcefully to urinate.
- A feeling of incomplete bladder emptying
- Difficulty starting urination
- Continuous dribbling of urine
- Due to this, patient is at risk of developing urinary tract infections, bladder stones, blood in urine, acute urinary retention.

रक्तग्रन्थि (*Granthi*)

रक्तं वातकफाद् दुष्टं बस्तिद्वारे सुदारूणम्।
ग्रन्थिं कुर्यात् स कृच्छ्रेण सृजेन्मूत्रं तदावृतम्।। अश्मरीसमशूलं तं रक्तग्रन्थिं प्रचक्षते।
(च.सि. 9/41)

When *Vata* and *Kapha Dosha* are afflicted by blood, they produce hard nodular mass in opening of urinary bladder. Because of this obstruction the patient passes urine with difficulty and pain in calculus. This is known as *Granthi* (*Raktagranthi*).

Related To Tumour:

There are different types of tumour developing in the urinary tract. They may indicate presence with following sign-symptoms:

- Blood/ blood clots in urine

- Pain/ burning sensation during urination
- Frequent urination with many times urination at night
- Lower backache (mostly one sided)

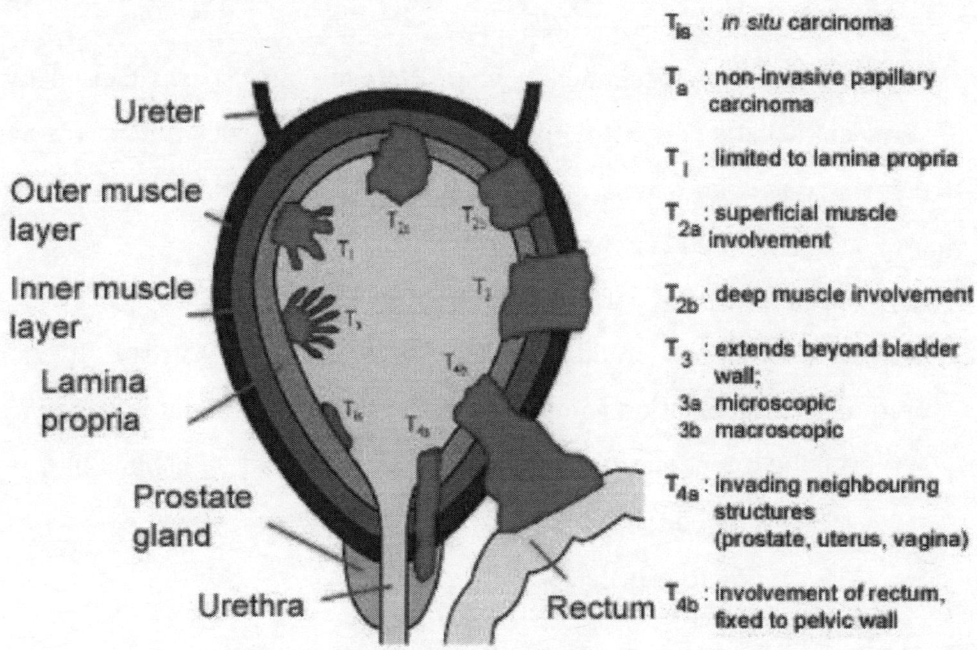

Figure: 7.2 Stages of Bladder Cancer

बस्तिकुण्डल (*Bastikundala*)

द्रुताध्वलङ्घनायासादभिघातात् प्रपीडनात्।स्वस्थानाद्बस्तिरूद्वृत्तः स्थूलस्तिष्ठति गर्भवत्।।
शूलस्पन्दनदाहार्तो बिन्दुं स्त्रवत्यपि। पीडितस्तु सृजेद्धारां संस्तम्भोद्वेष्टनार्तिमान्। (च.सि. 9/44)

Even during fast travelling, jumping, exertion and injury to lower region; the pressure in the urinary bladder bulges out from its place and stays in upward position. There is presence of quivering and burning sensation and pain. The urine comes out drop by drop and present with stiffness and cramps. It is compared with severe weapon and poison. This condition is called as *Bastikundala* and related with atonicity of bladder.

Atonic urinary bladder is a condition marked by a dilated, poorly contracting urinary bladder without evidence of lesion of central nervous system. A neurogenic bladder caused by destruction of sensory nerve fibers from bladder to spinal cord.

मूत्रौत्सङ्ग (*Mutrotsanga*)

मूत्रोत्संङ्गः स विच्छिन्नमुच्छेषगुरूशेफसः।
वाताकृतिर्भवेद्वातान्मूत्रे शुष्यति संक्षयः।। (च.सि. 9/34)

When due to derangement of channels and spasm caused by *Vata* some urine stays at the junction of glans penis and is passed out afterwards with severe pain or painlessly it is known as *Mutrotsanga* in which the patient passes the remnant urine is broken streams and heaviness in penis.

Clinical Features Of Stricture Of Urethra:

The hallmark sign of urethral stricture is a weak urinary stream. It can be result of injury, urethral instrumentation (transurethral resection of prostrate, bladder, endoscopic kidney surgery) and infection (like in Gonorrhea). Followed with signs like:

- Urinary frequency with urgency
- Straining to urinate
- Pain
- Urinary tract infections
- Prostratitis
- Inability to completely empty bladder

विड्घात (*Vidghata*)

मूत्रस्त्रोतः प्रपद्येत विट्संसृष्टं तदा नरः।
विड्गन्धं मूत्रयेत् कृच्छ्राद्विड्विघातं विनिर्दिशेत्।।
(च.सि. 9/43)

In case of *Vidghata,* when the subject is rough & debilitated person stool reversed in passage due to *Vata* enters into the urinary canal, he passes urine contaminated with feces and having fecal odour and with difficulty.

Fistula Developing In Urinary Tract:

Fistula here is an abnormal opening between urinary tract organs (kidneys, ureters, bladder & urethra). Urinary fistula can also form an abnormal connection between a urinary tract organ or with nearby structure like vagina, colon etc. and following types of fistula can be observed.

- A **vesicovaginal fistula** opens between the vagina and the bladder. This is the most frequent kind of urinary fistula in women. This occurs most often because of a previous hysterectomy.
- An **entero-vesical fistula** opens between the bladder and bowel. This is another of the most common urinary fistulas.
- A **vesico-uterine fistula** opens between the bladder and the uterus.
- A **uretero-vaginal fistula** opens between the vagina and ureter (the tube that carries urine between the kidneys and bladder). Most ureterovaginal fistulas occur because of prior hysterectomy or other pelvic surgery.
- A **urethra-vaginal fistula** opens between the vagina and the urethra.
- A **colo-vesical fistula** opens between the bladder and the colon.
- A **recto-vaginal fistula** opens between the vagina and the rectum.

Causes of Urinary Fistula:

Damage to the tissues of the urinary tract, pelvic region or vagina can create the conditions for a fistula. Urinary fistulas can develop from an injury or accident, a surgery, radiation treatment or (less often) by an infection.

Symptoms of Urinary Fistula

Fistulas usually are painless. Most people become aware that they have a fistula because of their symptoms. These symptoms might include:

- Fluid leaking from the vagina.
- Continual leakage of urine from the vagina.
- Foul-smelling gas or discharge from the vagina.
- Faeces leaking into the vagina.
- Frequent urinary tract infections (UTIs).
- Passing gas from the urethra while urinating.
- Abdominal pain.

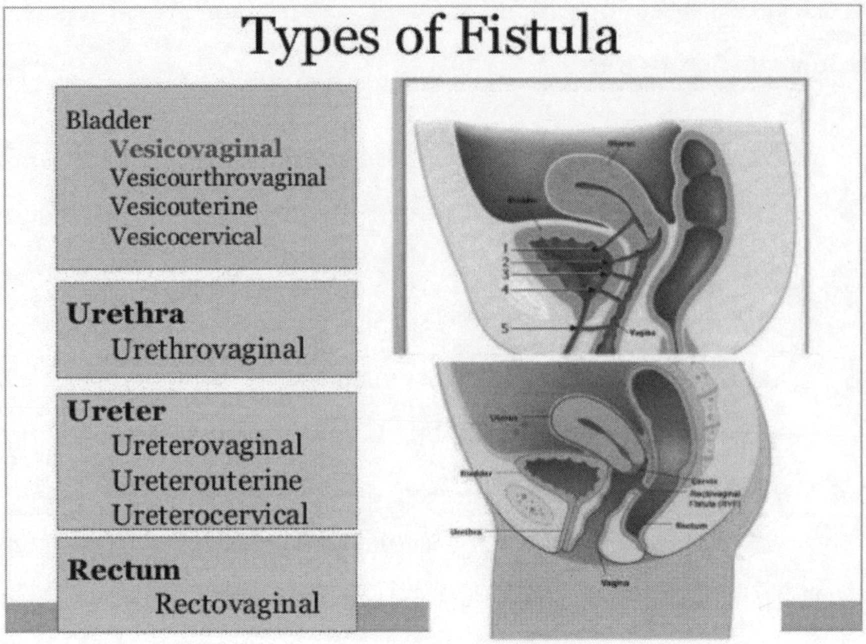

Figure 7.3 Types of Fistula

Applied aspect of diseases:

There are many related disorders which result in urinary tract pathology. If the prostate gland enlarges due to increase in cell proliferation (benign prostatic hyperplasia) the flow of urine is blocked, stones may form, result in urinary infections. The conditions like stricture of urethra, atonicity of bladder are common reasons for blocked urination, haematuria. The embryological defect in development of urethra, bladder may result in fistula communicating between rectum and uterus. In such cases the absence of uro genital septum is absent from where the development of urethra, bladder takes place.

Obstruction in the urinary tract is common and important because it increases the susceptibility to infection and stone formation. Obstruction can occur at any age, in either sex and it can be at any level– renal pelvis, ureters, urinary bladder, and urethra.

These types of obstruction at any of these anatomical locations may be intra luminal, intramural or extra mural. It can be unilateral, bilateral, partial-complete, sudden or insidious. Long standing chronic partial obstruction may cause various functional and anatomical abnormalities.

The three important sequel of obstruction for anatomical changes are hydronephrosis, hydro ureter and hypertrophy of urinary bladder. One of the important pathology is related to urolithiasis/ nephrolithiasis.

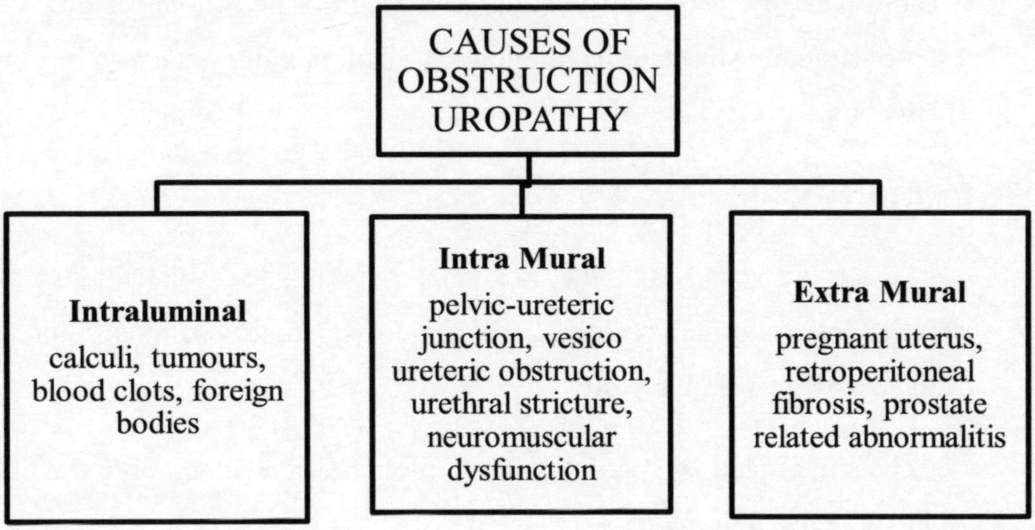

Flowchart: 7.1 Depicting Causes of Uropathy

Applied aspect:

The main signs present in the relation to excretory disorders are:

- Colic pain (renal colic): The main sign in **renal calculi,** characterized clinically by as they pass down along the ureters, manifested by haematuria.
- Haematuria: The presence of blood in the urine (haematuria) is abnormal & may be only indication of pathology in the urinary tract.

Types of pain:

- Fixed renal pain – located posteriorly in renal angle, worsen on movements.
- Ureteric colic pain - agonising pain in nature, passing from loin to groin region. It is often caused by stone entering the ureter but it may also occur due to lodging of stone at pelvic ureteric junction.

- The different types of stones like calcium oxalates, uric acid stones, mixed and cystine are present with various etiologies.

Inflammation and acute obstruction to flow of urine from the renal pelvis are liable to cause pain that is typically felt as deep seated ache in loin region. It is probably the result of stretching the capsule of kidney. Calculi in kidney can also be painful in absence of infection.

Ureteric colic:

This is an acute pain felt in loin & radiating to ipsilateral iliac fossa, genitals. Ureteric colic is usually caused by passage of a stone, but blood clot, sloughish renal papillae may give similar pain.

The site of pain is a partial guide to progress of a stone; more the pain radiates into groin, more distal the stone.

Calculi: Renal calculi are probably most common cause of acute obstruction leading to anuria.

Anuria:

It is defined as complete absence of urine production. Oliguria is present when less than 300mL of urine is excreted in a day. The condition can be due to obstruction, pelvic malignancy, surgery, retroperitoneal fibrosis or crystalluria.

Bladder stone: The primary stone is one that develops in sterile urine, it often originates in a kidney and passes down the ureters into the bladder, when it enlarges.

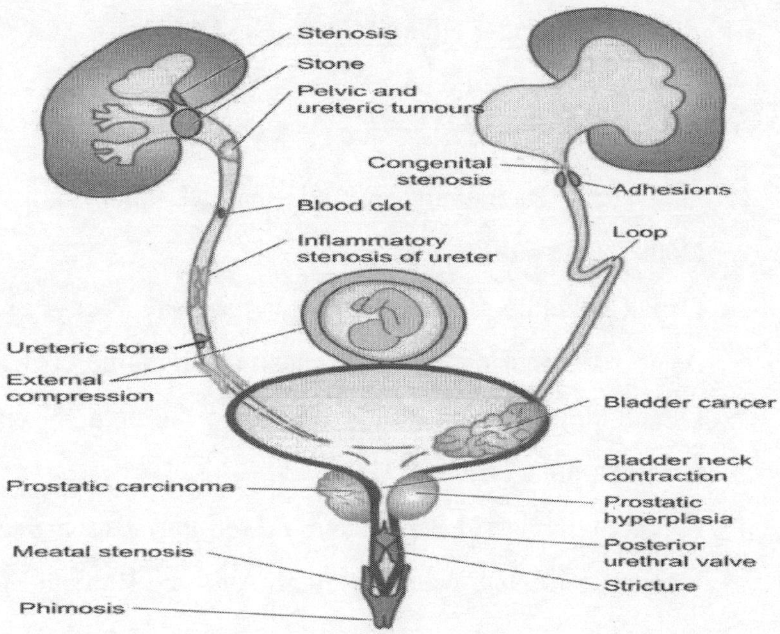

Fig: 7.2 Showing Causes of Obstructive Uropathy

KEYS POINTS:

- The process of excretion of urine (Mutra) is done via Basti (urinary bladder), Vrikka (kidneys) .
- Here only pathological condition creating anatomical changes are mentioned.
- Most of the anatomical change related to renal disorders is related to the pathway, situation of organ which is disturbed by various causes.

BIBLIOGRAPHY

REFERENCES FROM SAMHITAS:

1. Deva Raja Radhakant; Edited Shabdakalpadruma Vol 1-5, Reprint 1988 Delhi: Naga publishers.
2. Dr.D.G.Thatte; Edited Role of parental &environmental imprinting in Ayurveda; Reprint 2015, Varanasi: Chaukhambha Orientalia.
3. Dr. P.V.Sharma; Edited Charaka Samhita; Reprint 2010 Varanasi: Chaukhambha Orientalia.
4. Pandit Damodar Sharma Gaur; Edited Parishadya Shabadarth Shariram, 2nd Edition 1979 Nagpur: Baidyanath Ayurved Bhavan Ltd.
5. Pandit Kashinath Pandey and Dr. Gorakhnath Chaturvedi; Edited Charaka Samhita; Reprint 2009 Varanasi: Chaukhambha Bharati Academy.
6. R.K.Sharma and Bhagwan Das;Edited Charaka Samhita ; Reprint 2012 Varanasi: Chaukhambha Sanskrit Series Office.
7. Shri Manna Lal Abhimanyu; Edited Amar Singh Praneet Amarkosha; Reprint 2012, Varanasi: Chaukhamba Surbharti Prakashan
8. Shri Taranath; Edited Vachaspatyam Vol 1-6 3rd Edition 1970, Varanasi: Chowkhamba Sanskrit series.
9. Taranath Bhattacharya; Edited Shabadastom Mahanidhi
10. Vaidhya Harishchandra kushwaha; Edited Charaka Samhita ; Reprinted 2009; Varanasi: Chaukhambha Orientalia.
11. Vaidya Yadavji Trikamji; Edited Charaka Samhita Chakrapanidatta, Ayurveda Dipika Commentary, Reprint 2008 Varanasi: Chaukambha Surbharti Prakashan
12. Williams Monier Monier; Edited Sanskrit English dictionary 1st Edition, Reprint 1993 Delhi: Motilal Banarasidass Publishers.

MODERN LITERATURE:

1. Arthur C. Guyton, John E. Hall; Edited Textbook of Medical Physiology, 10th Edition 2003, Philadelphia: Imprint of Elsevier.
2. BD Chaurasia; Edited Human Anatomy 5th Edition; Reprint 2012: New Delhi;CBS Publishers & Distributors.
3. Byas Deb Ghosh ;Edited Human Anatomy for Students;2nd Edition; Reprint 2013; Jaypee brothers Publication
4. Dorlands; Pocket Medical Dictionary;29th Edition; Reprint 2013 India: Elsevier.
5. Gerard J. Tortora; Edited Principles of Anatomy and Physiology, 10th Edition, 2003, USA: John Wiley & Sons.
6. Harsh Mohan; Edited Textbook of Pathology;6th Edition 2010;Jaypee Brothers Publications.
7. Inderbir Singh and GP Pal; Edited Human Embryology; 9th Edition; Reprint 2013: MacMillan Publishers.
8. Keith L Moore; Edited Clinically Oriented Anatomy; 6th Edition 2010;Lippincott Williams & Wilkins.
9. K Sembulingum, Prema Sembulingam; Edited Essentials of Medical physiology, 6th Edition 2013, NewDelhi: Jaypee Brothers Medical Publishers.
10. Robbins, Kumar; Edited Basic Pathology; 7th Edition 2006, An imprint of Elsevier.
11. Susan Standring, Edited Gray's Anatomy, 39th edition 2008, Churchill Livingstone, Elsevier.
12. T.W Sadler; Edited Langmans Medical Embryology; 12th Edition; Reprint 2012:Lippincott Williams & Wilkins.
13. Vishram Singh; Edited Textbook of Clinical Embryology 1st Edition; Reprinted 2013; Elsevier.

JOURNALS:

- Pramod kumar Singh,NS Tripathi,PS Byadgi ; The Concept of Genetics in Ayurveda; AJMAMS: Volume 1; Issue 2; July-2012
- Saroja N,Ram Reddy GP,Venkata, Lavanya G;Concept of Vata Vs Nervous system;IJAM;Issue:2013

ABBREVATIONS USED

- च. सू : *Charaka Sutra Sthana*
- च. शा : *Charaka Shaarir Sthana*
- च. वि : *Charaka Vimana Sthana*
- च. चि : *Charaka Chikitsa Sthana*
- च. सि : *Charaka Sidhi Sthana*
- वा. : वाचस्पत्यम्
- श.क.द्रु. : शब्दकल्पद्रुम भाग
- अ.को. : अमरकाष
- वै. सु. : वैद्यकीय सुभाषितसाहित्यम्